VINTAGE
GREETING CARDS
WITH MARYJO MCGRAW

NORTH LIGHT BOOKS
Cincinnati, Ohio

WWW.ARTISTSNETWORK.COM

07 06 05 04 03   5 4 3 2 1

Library of Congress Cataloging-in-Publication Data
McGraw, MaryJo.
Vintage Greeting Cards with MaryJo McGraw.
  p. cm.
Includes index.
ISBN 1-58180-413-X (pbk. : alk. paper)
  1. Greeting cards. I. Title.

TT872.M3428 2003
745.594'1--dc21
                        2003046411

EDITOR: Jolie Lamping Roth
DESIGNER: Andrea Short
LAYOUT ARTIST: Karla Barker
PRODUCTION COORDINATOR: Michelle Ruberg
PHOTOGRAPHERS: Christine Polomsky and Al Parrish
PHOTO STYLIST: Jan Nickum

METRIC CONVERSION CHART		
TO CONVERT	TO	MULTIPLY BY
Inches	Centimeters	2.54
Centimeters	Inches	0.4
Feet	Centimeters	30.5
Centimeters	Feet	0.03
Yards	Meters	0.9
Meters	Yards	1.1
Sq. Inches	Sq. Centimeters	6.45
Sq. Centimeters	Sq. Inches	0.16
Sq. Feet	Sq. Meters	0.09
Sq. Meters	Sq. Feet	10.8
Sq. Yards	Sq. Meters	0.8
Sq. Meters	Sq. Yards	1.2
Pounds	Kilograms	0.45
Kilograms	Pounds	2.2
Ounces	Grams	28.4
Grams	Ounces	0.04

ABOUT THE AUTHOR

MaryJo McGraw is a nationally known rubber stamp artist and author whose work has been featured in leading rubber stamp enthusiast publications. Innovative techniques and creative teaching methods have made her a much sought-after instructor at conventions, retreats, cruises and stores for over fifteen years.

ACKNOWLEDGMENTS

To the whole gang at North Light!

You all make it so much fun I want to do at least a hundred books! Special thanks to Greg Albert, who found me; David Lewis, who keeps me thinking about the next GREAT book; Tricia Waddell, who keeps me thinking about the next REAL book; Sally Finnegan, who keeps me laughing; Christine Polomsky, who makes me look good; and Jolie Lamping Roth, who kept me on track and on time!

dedication

I WOULD LIKE TO DEDICATE THIS BOOK TO MY FAMILY AND FRIENDS, WHOSE PICTURES REMIND ME HOW PRECIOUS EVERY MOMENT REALLY IS.

table of contents

GETTING THE VINTAGE LOOK!

pg. **18**

INTRO

The look of heirloom papers, photos and ephemera has always held a certain fascination for me. There is no time better spent than a day rummaging through antique stores or flea markets searching for the odd embellishment or antique photograph.

After years of collecting, I have quite a nice stash. The problem is I never want to use the actual vintage items unless I have a huge collection of them. So I try to use tricks, techniques and a color copier or scanner to fool the eye of the card's recipient into thinking the items are the real thing.

In this book I have recreated the look I love, using items old and new, including ribbons, rickrack, buttons and my family's old photos (along with products that can alter their appearance).

I HOPE YOU'LL ENJOY MAKING A FEW OF THESE CARDS YOURSELF.

< TOOLS & MATERIALS >

Here is a description of the most common tools and materials used for the projects in this book. Feel free to add your own creative touches to your cards, and use the tools and materials you are most comfortable with.

PAPER

Always search out the best quality paper for your cards and projects. Paper is the first item that gets noticed on a greeting card, and if it is flimsy or feels cheap it reflects on you. For greeting cards in particular I prefer heavyweight cardstock.

In the paper world there are coated and uncoated stocks, and both have their place in card making. Coated stocks are generally smooth to the touch and can be glossy or smooth. There are even pearlized and shimmering coated cardstocks. Inks and paints tend to sit on the surface of these papers making it difficult to use pigment inks that need to dry by absorbing into the paper. Uncoated cardstock has a more toothy feel that inks and paints sink into. A beautiful watercolor paper is the perfect example of uncoated paper.

For a truly vintage-looking greeting, I like a heavy uncoated ivory cardstock. For cards that have a vintage flavor, I have used papers in heirloom colors that are both coated and uncoated.

TRANSLUCENT VELLUM

Translucent vellum is a sheer paper that is now available in many weights and colors. It has a matte feel and an elegant appearance. Translucent vellum also comes in ready-made envelopes, which are perfect for vintage greetings.

Another type of paper with a similar look to vellum is glassine, which is a waxy sheer paper. Glassine comes in several colors and is also available in many envelope sizes. There is also a variety of plastic papers that have a similar look but feel slick and are more modern looking.

ADHESIVES & MEDIUMS

Today there are many types of adhesives available, from old-fashioned pastes to new polymer mediums. In this book I have used several kinds.

DIAMOND GLAZE

Diamond Glaze is perhaps my favorite adhesive/medium. It can be used as a basic glue for paper when brushed on thin or as a heavy adhesive for three-dimensional embellishments. Since it is clear it is also excellent for shiny non-porous surfaces like mica tiles, acetate, beads and glitters. Diamond Glaze can also be used as a fixative over chalk and watercolor paint and crayons or it can create a vinyl look by simply brushing it evenly on paper or tissue. Finally it can be mixed with a huge array of inks, paints and dyes.

OMNI GEL

An excellent medium, Omni Gel is made specifically for photo transfers onto paper, fabric, metal, glass, leather and wood. It is also a great adhesive for heavy materials and is exceptionally good for non-porous items.

Diamond Glaze

MICROGLAZE

This super-fine wax is excellent as a fixative for many surfaces, including paper, polymer clays, leather and many mixed media projects. It can also be mixed with powdered pigments and buffed into surfaces such as paper. Since it leaves no oil ring on paper, it is a great resist wax to hold back paints and inks. The excess can be buffed away once the color has dried.

GEL MEDIUMS

Golden molding pastes, heavy or solid gels, and soft gels can be used on cards to change the textures and weight of paper, cardstock or chipboard. These mediums are created to be used with paints, inks and other colorants. They can often be used as an adhesive in collage projects and can be especially good at holding three-dimensional pieces on paper. Gel mediums can also be used to transfer color copies from paper to other surfaces as well.

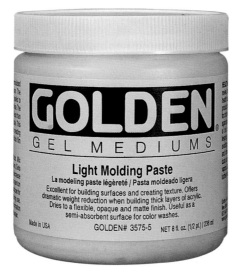

Molding Paste

DOUBLESTICK TAPES

Doublestick tapes are invaluable card-making accessories. A double-sided paper-lined tape is what I use on most projects since it can be torn and cut into usual shapes and sizes. There are several brands of clear doublestick tape that I keep on hand for projects that are sheer (like vellum). I also keep repositionable tape ready for those times when you could use an extra hand.

BEESWAX

Different types of wax have long been used as adhesives. You can brush melted beeswax over pictures and artwork to adhere and protect the surface. Once the wax has set, it can be scraped to any thickness and even buffed to a soft sheen. While the wax is warm, try stamping images into the surface to create decorative patterns. Embellishment items added to the hot wax create added texture. Remember to be very careful when using beeswax, so you don't burn yourself.

POLYMER CLAY

Polymer clays are great for paper projects since they are lightweight and can be rolled very thin. Polymer clays can be sanded and even trimmed with scissors when rolled thin. There are many types of polymer clays and all will work for these projects with slightly varied results. I prefer Premo for my projects because it remains slightly flexible and does not become brittle over time.

ANTIQUING & STAINING MEDIUMS

To achieve a vintage look, there are several mediums available.

WALNUT INK

This ink is especially good for antique coloring since it is a rich cocoa brown. Walnut ink comes in two varieties: liquid and crystals. I prefer the crystals since they allow a wider range of looks. The amount of hot water added to the crystals alters the depth of color from a deep dark stain to a pale watercolor-like effect. The crystals themselves can be sprinkled on wet paper for interesting effects as well.

There are imitation walnut inks on the market that are made from peat instead of walnut. This ink also has a unique look, but has a bit of a greenish tint rather than the true brown of the real walnut ink.

SHOE POLISH

A great antiquing medium for the vintage look is shoe polish. Shoe polish is still around in many forms. In this book I use the old-fashioned paste wax polishes that come in a few colors as well as neutral, which is excellent for resist techniques. Creme shoe polish can also be used, but the color is more intense, so start slowly on a test patch and use less.

GOLDEN FLUID ACRYLICS

These are the perfect acrylics to use on paper. They are quick drying and translucent, and do not warp the paper surface like heavier acrylic products. These paints can be dry-brushed onto paper to create beautiful backgrounds. They are also excellent for staining surfaces. Fluid acrylics come in a huge array of colors and can be mixed with any mediums.

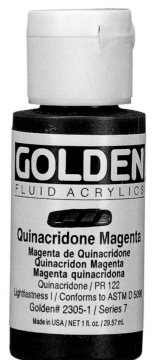

Fluid Acrylics

Japanese Screw Punch

TOOLS

There are several tools that will be helpful when making your vintage greeting cards.

BONE FOLDER

A bone folder is a book-binding tool used to score and crease papers. It is a smooth tool shaped like a letter opener and made out of bone (hence the name), wood or resin.

CRAFT KNIFE

A craft knife is one of the most important tools in a card maker's kit. I still refer to what is known as a No. 11 size knife with a soft grip handle, but there are many styles available today including retractable pen knives, which are very safe. Change the blades often to ensure clean and easy cutting.

JAPANESE SCREW PUNCH

This wonderful tool is technically a bookbinder's instrument that fits well in any paper fanatic's kit. With it you can punch various-size holes in any paper, leather, clay or even thin metal surface. This amazing tool will punch through many layers at a time, which is why bookbinders love it!

I use this on all projects where I need to punch through several layers at once. There are punches that can be hammered through several layers, and on some surfaces a regular handheld hole punch will work.

Color Dusters

INKS & APPLICATORS

Vintage doesn't have to mean brown. There are a wide range of inks and applicators that make it easy to add color.

PIÑATA COLORS

Piñata Colors are very pigmented alcohol inks that leave brilliant color on non-porous surfaces. These inks come in a great range of color, are inexpensive and are perfect on three-dimensional embellishment items like buttons, mica, hardware and more. These inks can be used to color acetate as well.

Piñata Color

CLARO EXTENDER

This extender is specifically made for extending alcohol ink without diluting the color.

COLOR DUSTERS

Mini stippling brushes for paints, pastel chalks, inks and more, Color Dusters are a great inexpensive tool for applications of all kinds on paper.

LEAFING PENS

Leafing pens come in a variety of colors, including gold, copper and silver. These particular pens are an excellent way to edge, touch up and decorate paper, mica tiles, foil ephemera, beads, buttons and much more. Leafing pens work on paper, cardstock, cardboard and non-porous surfaces, and when several layers are applied, it truly looks like metal. Other types of paint pens will do an effective job but will not have the same rich look.

Leafing Pen

CARD EMBELLISHMENTS

Be creative when embellishing your cards. Everyday items found in a junk drawer can make terrific add-ons to cards. Here are some of my favorite embellishments.

SMALL HARDWARE

Many small hardware items, such as eyelets, solid heads, brads and typewriter key frames, have become widely available in paper, scrapbook and stamp stores, as well as local chain craft stores. I especially like the very tiny brass brads. The notions department in sewing stores is also a good area to check for these and other small embellishment items.

Many of these metal items can be attached to paper with a small hammer and a setting tool. In the case of the typewriter key frames, a small hammer is all you will need.

MICA TILES, CHIPS AND GLITTER

Mica is an iridescent mineral that can be pulled apart into thin sheets. These sheets can be used for almost any application where acetate is used to add a vintage look to many surfaces. When cut down into chips or glitter, mica gives an antique look over paper, wax or other media that are preferred over standard mylar glitters.

PAPER FOIL EPHEMERA

Antique embossed foil papers can be difficult to come by. Luckily there are companies now that replicate the look for a decent price. Be careful when using foil ephemera, as the embossing laminates several pieces tightly together. Slowly pull apart the layers because this paper is easily torn.

Paper Foil Ephemera

Mica Tiles

Miscellaneous Embellishments

13

< BASIC TECHNIQUES >

There are always a few basic techniques that are important to learn at the beginning of any project. Play with these basics before diving into a full project to practice and have a little fun! Also check out the basic information and great tips for working with the specialty materials like walnut ink and beeswax described on page 11.

STAMPING BASICS

There are three basic types of inks: pigment, dye and solvent. All three are used in this book. As a simple rule of thumb, here is how each works: Dye ink dries through evaporation on porous surfaces like paper. It fades over time in most cases.

Pigment dries by absorption and in some cases by heat. Pigment is a thicker, more opaque ink than the other types.

Solvents are made to dry on all surfaces, porous or non-porous. Solvents are transparent in appearance, much like dyes. In this book a particular ink is specified for each project.

The majority of ink pads in use today are the raised surface type. These are easiest to ink properly since the ink pad is applied to a rubber stamp. Old-fashioned pads are made of felt and covered in linen.

STEP ONE
Ink the stamp.

STEP TWO
Press the stamp to the paper using firm and even pressure, then lift.

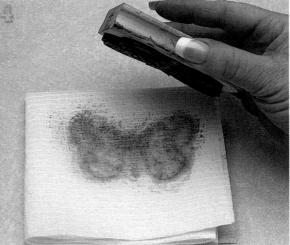

STEP THREE

Clean your stamp with a good strong cleaner. A good cleaner will have a conditioning agent in it to keep the stamp surface soft and pliable. You can also use products like baby wipes or window cleaners to clean the stamp, but they will not condition it. I prefer a solvent-type cleaner with a conditioner since it will remove all types of ink and paint.

STEP FOUR

After applying the cleaner, allow it to penetrate the surface. Wipe the surface of the stamp well with a paper towel or an old terry cloth towel.

SPECIALTY INKS

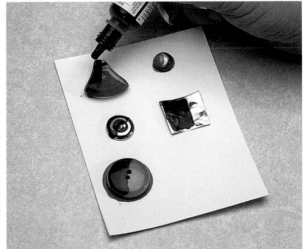

WALNUT INK

In this book, to achieve a vintage look on many of the projects, I have used walnut ink. This ink has a look that is not easily duplicated with other inks or paints. It is available in liquid or granular crystal form. The liquid is usually a medium-strength color, which can be diluted. The granular form is what I prefer since it can be adjusted to any strength with hot water, or used as a powder on wet surfaces.

PIÑATA COLOR

Piñata Color is an alcohol-based (solvent-based) ink that can be applied to a huge array of surfaces including glass, paper, polymer clay, plastics, mica and metals. Simply add a drop of this ink to a button or plastic bead. It can also be brushed like paint on larger surfaces.

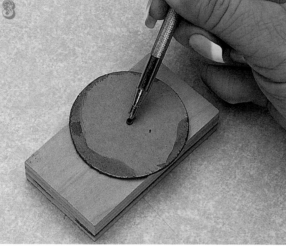

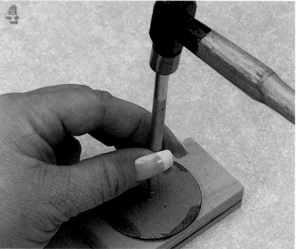

SETTING EYELETS

Eyelets create a professional look to cards and paper projects if they are set correctly. The right setting tool is the key. Look for a setter with a nipple end rather than the widely used cone shape. Use as small a hammer as you can find. A heavier hammer can apply too much pressure and smash the eyelet.

STEP ONE
Using a screw punch, awl or tiny hole punch, punch a hole for the eyelet. Check for the correct size of punch for the eyelets chosen.

STEP TWO
Insert the eyelet into the hole.

STEP THREE
Turn over the piece and insert the setting tool into the eyelet.

STEP FOUR
With the setting tool in place, tap evenly and firmly a few times with a small hammer.

Remove the setting tool, and with the hammer, tighten and finish the back of the eyelet with a few light taps.

COLOR-COPYING PHOTOS

All of the vintage photos in this book have been color copied using carbon-based toner. In many cases your scanner will work for simple projects that are only to be cut out and glued on a surface. For the projects that require the photo to be transferred from paper to a different type of surface, carbon-based copies must be used. Most good office supply stores and many printers can do the job for you. I have all my photos copied onto large paper that I can store for later use.

Black-and-white photos tend to have a gray appearance when simply copied as is. I usually ask for an 8 to 10 percent yellow screen to be added over the photo to give it some warmth. A good professional can help with this. You can also scan the photos at home and adjust the color to your liking on the computer before taking them to be copied.

8 percent yellow screen

10 percent yellow screen

12 percent yellow screen

GETTING THE VINTAGE LOOK!

This is the how-to part of the book containing 23 step-by-step cards, featuring a vintage look or antique quality created with a few simple techniques and plenty of fun embellishments. I have used a variety of materials, and most are available at your local art, craft, hardware, stamp or scrapbook store. Many of the embellishment items are from my own collection, and I am sure you have a similar stash of your own in a shoe box somewhere.

If you are just starting out collecting, look in antique, thrift and junk stores as well as online and at garage sales. I am exceptionally lucky finding sewing notions! Always buy the whole sewing, hat or shoe box full of goodies and keep an eye out for the stuffed grab bag. You certainly do not need the exact embellishment items to complete these projects. Substitute anything of a similar size, shape or texture.

USE THOSE IDEAS THAT POP INTO YOUR HEAD WHILE CREATING—AFTER ALL IT'S ONLY PAPER!

MATERIALS LIST

- copy of black-and-white photograph
- stiff brush (stencil or stippling brush)
- brown shoe polish
- paper towels
- two bamboo paper clips (online or in many stamp stores)
- doublestick tape
- complementary paper
- word stamp
- black ink
- dark folded cardstock

POINT OF ORIGIN

Aging and protecting color copies of favorite photos is simple using this shoe polish technique. Old-fashioned paste shoe polish is especially effective because it is a light buffing wax with a small amount of colored pigment. I apply it to black-and-white copies, yet it can also be used to age a wide array of paper products. Always test a small patch to see the effect on different weights and textures of papers.

TECHNIQUE:
Shoe Polish Overlay

CREATIVE MATERIAL:
bamboo clips

< POINT OF ORIGIN >

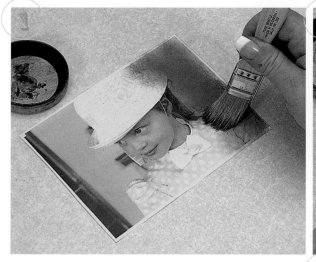

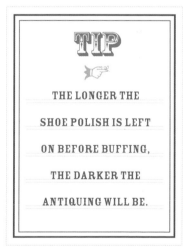

STEP ONE

This is a black-and-white photo that has been copied on the standard setting. Using a quick up-and-down motion with a stiff brush, apply a small amount of brown shoe polish to the photo. A stippling or stencil brush is perfect for this technique.

STEP TWO

Once the copy is completely covered with polish, buff and blend the polish with your fingers or a paper towel.

STEP THREE

For a bit of embellishment I added two bamboo paper clips to the top of the piece. Secure the clips with a piece of doublestick tape.

> **TIP**
>
> THE LONGER THE
> SHOE POLISH IS LEFT
> ON BEFORE BUFFING,
> THE DARKER THE
> ANTIQUING WILL BE.

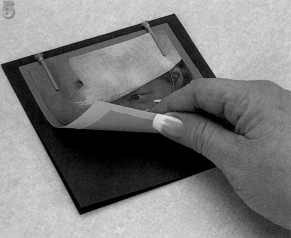

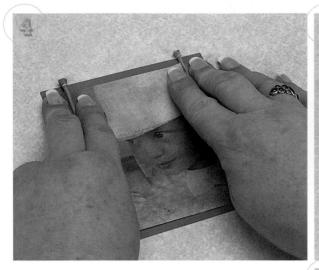

TIP

👉

USE WORDS CUT FROM

A THRIFT STORE

BOOK OR DICTIONARY

INSTEAD OF A STAMP.

STEP FOUR

Using a bit more doublestick tape, apply the copy to a layer of complementary paper.

STEP FIVE

Apply doublestick tape to the back of the piece, then center on dark folded cardstock.

STEP SIX

Stamp a word or two along the bottom of the copy in black ink.

Martini Time

The removable border band holds the card together.
The band is easy to make using doublestick tape for
an adhesive. The tape also makes it easy to remove
the band and open the card.

To protect color copies apply a thin layer of
neutral shoe polish then buff away the excess. This
waterproofs as well.

< V I P >

Walnut ink is another easy way to antique paper and other porous surfaces. This ink has a very rich color quality that is hard to duplicate with other inks or paints. While it is not widely available, it is easily found through specialty stamp and calligraphy stores, the Internet and mail-order art supply houses. I prefer the granules to premixed liquid, since the granules can be mixed in different strengths or used by themselves on wet surfaces.

TECHNIQUE:
Walnut Ink

CREATIVE MATERIALS:
ticket stub, game pieces, rickrack

MATERIALS LIST

- walnut ink
- soft brush
- scrap paper
- spray water bottle
- watercolor paper
- yellow or gold folded cardstock
- rickrack
- paper towels
- color-copied photo (or scanned photo)
- photo corners
- doublestick tape
- old ticket stub
- game pieces
- Diamond Glaze (or epoxy or super glue)

ADMIT ONE
To The Hulman Terrace.

ADMIT ONE
To The Grounds

1 STEP ONE

Mix up three small dishes of walnut ink in varied strengths. (Steps 1–5 show how to vary the ink strength. You will need a very deep brown, a medium brown and a light brown for the card.) Place one teaspoon of the granules into a small glass dish.

2 STEP TWO

Add in two teaspoons of hot water and mix until dissolved.

3 STEP THREE

Using a piece of scrap paper, apply a very deep brown mixture of walnut ink to the paper.

TIP

IF YOU DON'T WANT TO CREATE
OR STORE SEVERAL SHADES OF
INK, START WITH A LIGHT MIX-
TURE AND LAYER THE INK, WAIT-
ING FOR EACH LAYER TO DRY
BEFORE APPLYING THE NEXT.

TIP

CONTINUE IN THIS FASHION

UNTIL YOU HAVE ACHIEVED THE

TONES OF INK THAT YOU LIKE.

ALL OF THE INK CAN BE SAVED

AND STORED IN AIRTIGHT

BOTTLES OR JARS. MARK EACH

WITH A LABEL COLORED WITH

THE INK INSIDE.

STEP FOUR

Spray the walnut ink with plain water while it is still wet to lighten it. Set aside to dry.

STEP FIVE

Add two teaspoons more of the hot water for a weaker solution.

STEP SIX

Once you have made the three strengths of ink, use a soft brush to spread a medium mixture of walnut ink onto a piece of watercolor paper. Let dry.

TIP
☞
MUSLIN, RIBBON AND
MOST NATURAL FIBER
CAN BE DYED WITH
WALNUT INK.

STEP SEVEN

Apply a light brown mixture of walnut ink with a soft brush to both sides of a yellow or gold piece of cardstock. The cardstock here is pearlized, which adds interest. Set aside to dry.

STEP EIGHT

I have decided to use rickrack for the trim. It is easy to antique with walnut ink. Dip the trim into the strongest solution of ink.

STEP NINE

Place the trim onto several layers of paper towel. Spray sections of the trim with water to lighten. This will create a more natural aged look. Allow the trim to dry thoroughly.

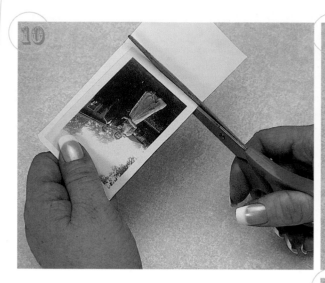

STEP TEN
Trim a color copy or scanned photo leaving a $\frac{1}{4}$" (6mm) border all the way around the photo.

STEP ELEVEN
Add photo corners to the trimmed photo. Moisten the photo corners with water before adding to the antiqued watercolor paper.

STEP TWELVE
Using doublestick tape, add the photo to the antiqued watercolor paper layer.

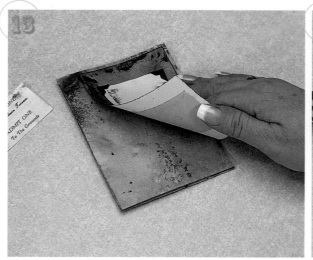

STEP THIRTEEN

Layer the watercolor paper and photo onto the folded cardstock (from step 7).

STEP FOURTEEN

Add all of the embellishments. Tie on the rickrack. Use double-stick tape to add the ticket to the front.

Glue must be used for the game pieces. Diamond Glaze takes a while to dry, but it holds heavy items on paper very well. Epoxy and super glues also will work.

TIP

PHOTO CORNERS ARE
NOW WIDELY AVAILABLE AT
SCRAPBOOK AND STAMP
STORES, AS WELL AS LARGE
CRAFT CHAINS. I PREFER THE
SIMPLE BLACK ONES FOR
MOST PROJECTS, ALTHOUGH
WHITE CORNERS THAT HAVE
BEEN AGED LOOK GREAT TOO.

< SEA GLASS MEMORIES >

Whether you find it on the beach or at the craft store, this is a great way to use a frosty piece of sea glass. Add the sea glass to a walnut ink colored card with an heirloom-looking ribbon and you have a quick and easy card full of memories. The quick addition of a foil embellishment sets off the edges of the sea glass.

TECHNIQUE:
Walnut Ink

CREATIVE MATERIALS:
sea glass, antique-style ribbon

MATERIALS LIST

- color-copied photo
- piece of sea glass
- clear glue
- silver leafing pen
- spray water bottle
- heavy cardstock
  (or watercolor paper)
- walnut ink granules
- stiff brush
- paper towel
- scoring tool
- antique-style ribbon
- gold foil flower

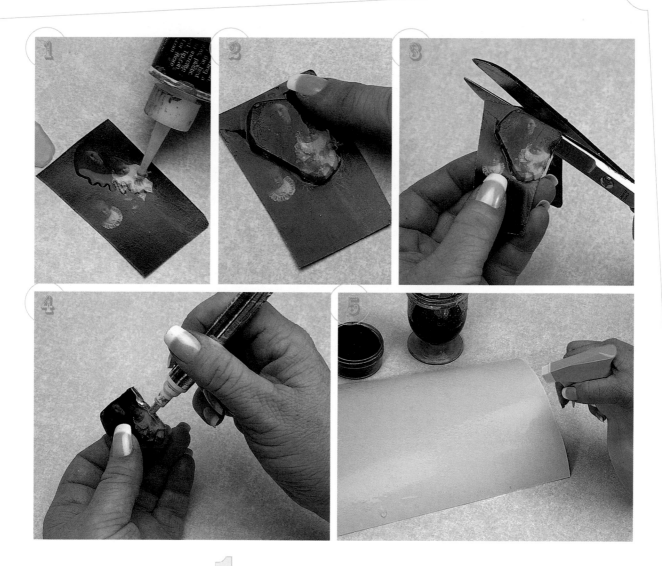

STEP ONE
Glue a color-copied photo to the back of a large piece of sea glass. A clear glue is best.

STEP TWO
To eliminate some of the frosted look so that the picture can be seen, add a drop or two of the same clear glue to the top of the sea glass. Let dry.

STEP THREE
Trim the excess paper from the sea glass.

STEP FOUR
Apply a silver leafing pen to the edges of the glass. Set aside to dry.

STEP FIVE
Spritz plain water on a piece of heavy cardstock or watercolor paper.

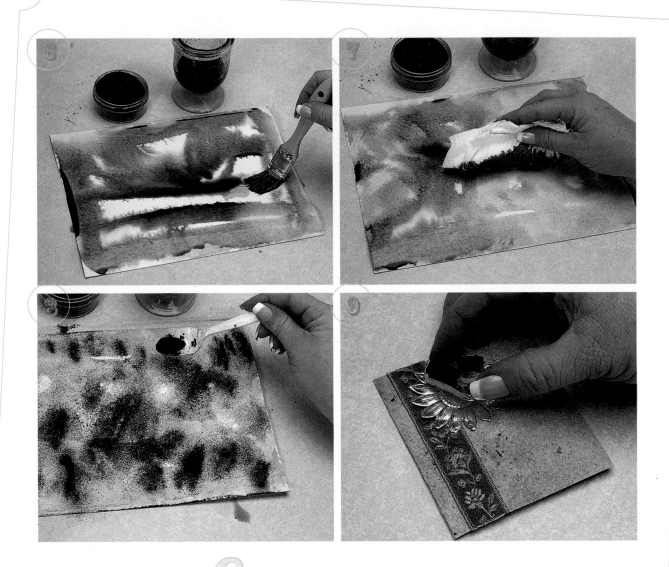

STEP SIX

Using a stiff brush, spread on a medium brown mixture of walnut ink (see pages 25–26 for information on mixing different ink strengths).

STEP SEVEN

Blot sections of the paper with a paper towel. You can also achieve some interesting looks using crunched up plastic instead of a paper towel.

STEP EIGHT

For a speckled look, apply some of the dry granules of walnut ink to any wet spots. Let dry, then brush away any excess granules.

STEP NINE

Cut the cardstock to the desired size. Score and fold. Since this ribbon is very heavy, I used a small amount of glue to adhere it to the cardstock. Use clear glue to position a gold foil flower onto the card, then add the sea glass.

Colored Sea Glass

Foil pieces are easy embellishments. This foil piece was cut in half lengthwise, with space left between the two pieces when glued to the card. The sea glass was placed in the middle of the embellishment.

33

Triple Threat

Use both light and dark photos to provide contrast. Notice the high contrast between the two lighter pieces with the darker piece in the middle. The white background adds to the intensity and helps show the vintage quality of the photos beneath the glass.

MATERIALS LIST

- rubber stamp and stamp pad (or a color-copied photo)
- cardstock
- MicroGlaze (or a light clear paste wax or a neutral shoe polish)
- walnut ink
- brush
- paper towels
- folded cardstock
- doublestick tape
- rusted metal corners
- clear glue

Using a light clear wax like MicroGlaze, or even a neutral shoe polish, is a great way to keep color in its place. When using the wax–resist technique, it is a good idea to do a test piece just to get the hang of where to apply the wax. Rusted metal accents are perfect embellishments for this monochromatic look.

TECHNIQUE:
Wax Resist

‹ ANCIENT EDGE ›

> ## TIP
>
> 👉
>
> IF YOU TEAR THE
> PAPER TOWARD YOU,
> A VERY ROUGH EDGE
> REMAINS. FOR A MORE
> SMOOTH EDGE, TEAR
> THE PAPER AWAY
> FROM YOU.

STEP ONE
Photocopy or stamp an image onto cardstock. Tear away the excess paper.

STEP TWO
Apply MicroGlaze to the parts of the copy that are to remain light. Start with a small amount and work it into the surface of the paper.

STEP THREE
Brush on the walnut ink. The rough torn edges pick up more ink and will be much darker.

TIP
☞

RUSTED METAL

EMBELLISHMENTS

ARE AVAILABLE AT

MANY CRAFT, PAPER

AND STAMP STORES.

STEP FOUR

Wipe off the excess ink and wax with a paper towel. Buff the piece again with a clean paper towel.

STEP FIVE

To waterproof, add another thin layer of wax to the whole piece.

STEP SIX

After adhering the piece to folded cardstock with doublestick tape, add rusted metal corners with a small amount of clear glue.

Hats Off

This background is created by using the wax-resist technique on uncoated cream-colored paper. I used thick watercolor paint instead of walnut ink to vary the color. The metal-rimmed tag was dipped in beeswax.

FLUID TIME

There are many types of solvents, including nail polish remover and many kinds of alcohol, that can transfer images from copier paper to cardstock. I like the way this stamp cleaner works. Many solvents and alcohols will not need heat—simply let them dry on their own. When working with solvents, alcohols or even smelly paints and inks, I prefer to be outside so that I do not have to be concerned with ventilation. If you must be indoors, keep the windows open and the fan running!

TECHNIQUE:
Liquid Photo Transfer

CREATIVE MATERIALS:
plastic watch crystal, mica flakes

MATERIALS LIST

- color-copied photos
- coated paper
- stamp cleaner (or nail polish remover or alcohol)
- heat gun (or hair dryer)
- bright-colored ink pad
- rubber stamp
- foil embellishments
- clear glue
- folded cardstock
- doublestick tape
- button
- plastic watch crystal
- assorted Piñata Colors (alcohol inks)
- brush (or sponge)
- Claro Extender
- mica flakes (or glitter)

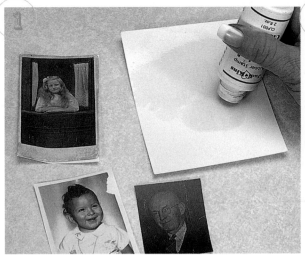

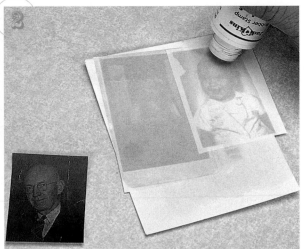

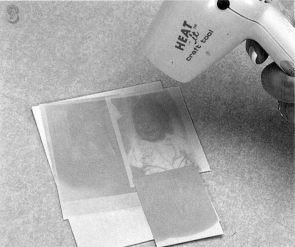

TIP

👉

MANILA SHIPPING

TAGS WORK ESPECIALLY

WELL FOR TRANSFERS

SINCE MANILA IS A

COATED PAPER.

STEP ONE

Choose and trim the color-copied photos. I have found that coated papers tend to work best for transfers, so use a coated cardstock for the card. Float the stamp cleaner completely over the surface of the coated paper.

STEP TWO

Lay the color copies face down into the stamp cleaner on the coated paper, then coat the back of each copy with the stamp cleaner.

STEP THREE

To speed the drying process, use a heat gun or hair dryer.

STEP FOUR

Remove the copies as soon as the pieces are dry. Do not let the paper cool or sit too long, as it will become difficult to remove. Afterward the image can be a bit sticky. Simply allow it to dry for a few minutes before moving on.

STEP FIVE

Now that everything has transferred, apply a little color to the paper using a brightly colored ink pad.

STEP SIX

A few stamped images are a nice addition to the open spaces.

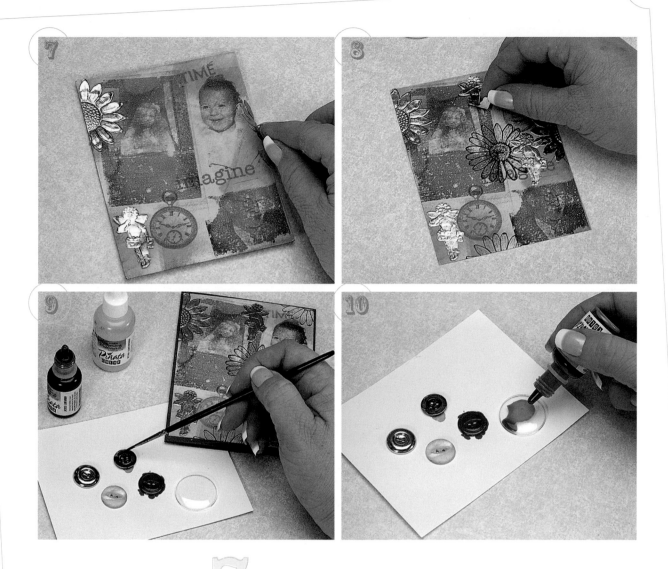

STEP SEVEN

Glue on a few foil embellishments.

STEP EIGHT

Trim the piece as necessary. Add a few more foil pieces, then apply the paper to folded cardstock with doublestick tape.

STEP NINE

There are a couple more embellishments to add: the button and a plastic watch crystal. These knick-knacks needed a color change, though, to fit the look of the card. Piñata Colors (alcohol inks) will color these items quite easily. Just apply a drop and then move it around with a brush or sponge. These inks are vividly colored and will stain your fingers, so always use a brush or sponge to apply.

STEP TEN

Add orange Piñata Color to the watch crystal.

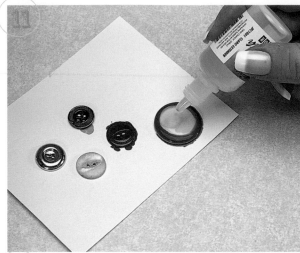

STEP ELEVEN

To lighten the ink in the center of the crystal, add a drop or two of Claro Extender. This will enable the picture beneath to be seen more clearly.

STEP TWELVE

Add a small amount of glue to the rim of the crystal and to each of the buttons.

STEP THIRTEEN

Position all of the three-dimensional embellishments.

STEP FOURTEEN

If there is any glue peeking out, add a few mica flakes or glitter to cover it.

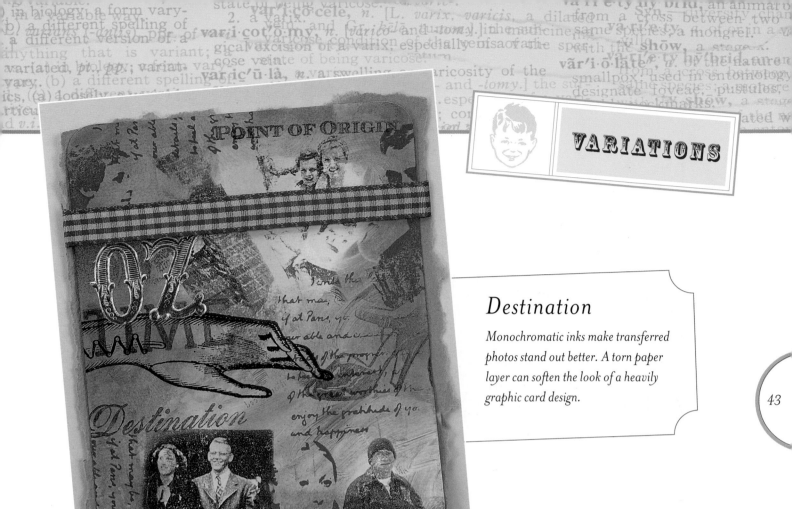

Destination

Monochromatic inks make transferred photos stand out better. A torn paper layer can soften the look of a heavily graphic card design.

43

Monochrome

Using the card recipient's initials is a nice, personal touch. Corner rounders and punches are excellent embellishment tricks for very large cards.

MATERIALS LIST

- family photos with small faces
- copper washer
- craft knife
- metal stamping alphabet set
- metallic copper-toned paper
- small, heavy hammer
- dark shoe polish
- paper towels
- Diamond Glaze
- ruler
- rust-colored folded cardstock
- Omni Gel (or thick multi-purpose glue that works with metal)
- antique-style ribbon
- old watch face
- tiny face plate

I found some copper washers and thought I would create jewelry with them. Instead one found its way onto this charming card. Copper is a soft metal and is very easy to impress with metal stamps. Copper is also a great metal to patina.

TECHNIQUE:
Stamped Metal

CREATIVE MATERIALS:
copper washer, old watch face, antique-style ribbon, tiny face plate

PRECIOUS

MEMORY WINDOW

STEP ONE

Look for little heads in family photos, then have them copied onto one sheet. Select one that fits into the center of the washer. Using a craft knife, cut out the head leaving at least ⅛" (3mm) all the way around. Set aside.

STEP TWO

Metal stamping sets are available at many small hardware and stamp stores, and online. This particular one is very tiny. Copper is great to stamp into because it is so soft. Stamp out a word by positioning each letter perpendicular to the surface of the washer. Hit the top of the stamp with a small, heavy hammer. Two or three good strong taps should do the trick.

STEP THREE

Put a small amount of dark shoe polish onto the letters using a craft knife.

TIP

WHEN STAMPING WORDS INTO
METAL OR PAPER, COUNT OUT
THE LETTERS, START WITH THE
CENTER LETTER AND WORK
YOUR WAY OUT TO EACH SIDE.
THIS IS THE SURE WAY TO GET
A WORD CENTERED.

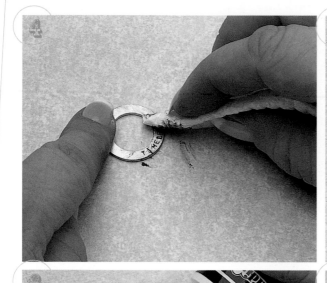

STEP FOUR

Rub the polish into the stamped letters with a paper towel. Buff off the excess.

STEP FIVE

Place the washer over the cut photo. Begin to fill the interior of the washer with Diamond Glaze.

STEP SIX

Completely fill the interior of the washer with Diamond Glaze and let dry thoroughly.

STEP SEVEN

Trim the excess paper using a craft knife or scissors.

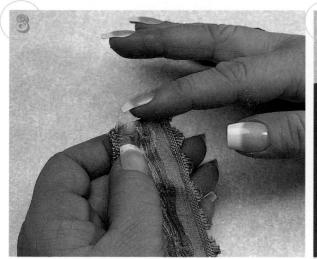

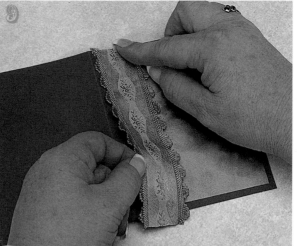

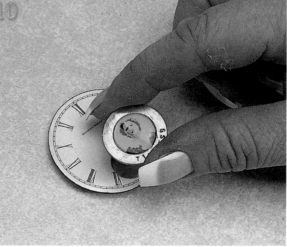

STEP EIGHT

Prepare the card by layering a metallic copper-toned paper piece on the front of rust-colored cardstock. Add glue to the back of the ribbon.

STEP NINE

Glue a heavy antique-looking ribbon to the front of the card.

STEP TEN

An old watch face is an excellent accompaniment to the washer. If you cannot find a real one, a paper one will do. Glue the washer to the watch. You will need a thick multipurpose glue that works with metal. Omni Gel is a good choice.

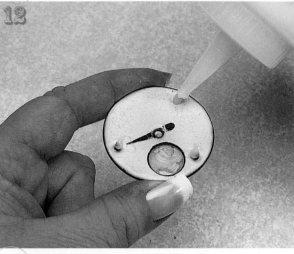

STEP ELEVEN
Add the tiny face plate on top of the washer.

STEP TWELVE
Add the Omni Gel to the back of the watch face.

STEP THIRTEEN
Lay the piece on the front of the card. Let dry.

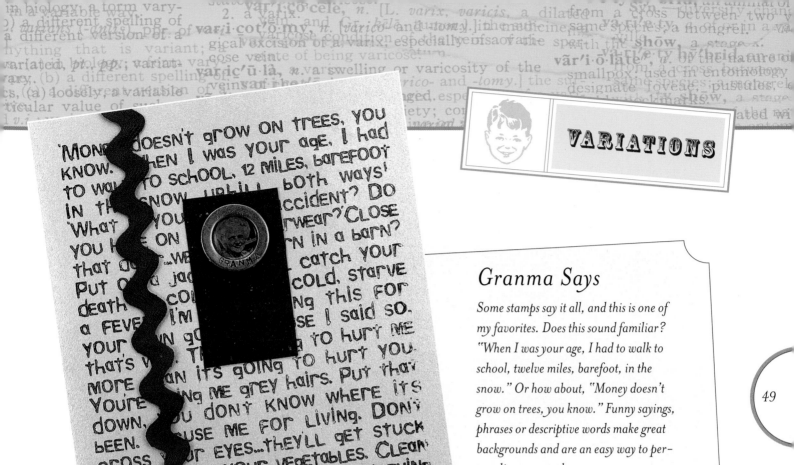

'MONEY DOESN'T GROW ON TREES, YOU KNOW. WHEN I was YOUR aGe, I had to walk TO SCHOOL, 12 MILES, BAREFOOT IN THE SNOW, UPHILL BOTH ways! 'What's YOUR... ACCIDENT? DO YOU HAVE ON... UNDERWEAR? CLOSE that door, WE... BORN IN a barN? Put On a jac... catch YOUR death of COLD, starve to death... I'M... doing this FOR a FEVER... BECAUSE I said SO. YOUR OWN GOOD... TO HURT ME more than its going to hurt YOU. that's Why... THIS is GIVING ME grey hairs. Put that... YOU don't KNOW where its YOURE down, YOU... Excuse ME FOR LiVing. DON'T been. ...Your EYES...THEY'LL GET STUCK cross... Eat YOUR VEGETABLES. CLEAN that... THINK OF aLL THE STARVINg YOUR PL... DON'T GET SMArT WITH ME. children... DaY is CHILDREN's DaY. Every... THE NEIGHBORS THINK? WHAT WILL

Granma Says

Some stamps say it all, and this is one of my favorites. Does this sound familiar? "When I was your age, I had to walk to school, twelve miles, barefoot, in the snow." Or how about, "Money doesn't grow on trees, you know." Funny sayings, phrases or descriptive words make great backgrounds and are an easy way to per-sonalize your card.

Sweet Sunflower

The foil embellishment underneath the washer helps create the sunflower image. You can also place the ribbon under-neath the flower to create a stem.

< NAPKIN >

Napkins these days are beautifully printed with artwork that is perfectly sized for greeting cards. I look for vintage-looking napkins or imagery that can be cut out easily. Also look for Japanese tea napkins. These napkins are great because the rice paper is thin and easy to collage. Choose a heavy cardstock for this card because the typewriter key frame spikes are easier to use on firmer paper. Typewriter key frames may be tricky to find, so check out the Resources on page 126.

CREATIVE MATERIALS:
*vintage-style napkin,
metal typewriter key frame,
an old playing card*

MATERIALS LIST

- vintage-looking napkin or imagery
- brush
- clear glue
- heavy cardstock
- bone folder (or ruler)
- gift wrap flower cutouts
- old playing card
- color-copied photo
- metal typewriter key frame
- black permanent marker
- gold leafing pen
- small hammer

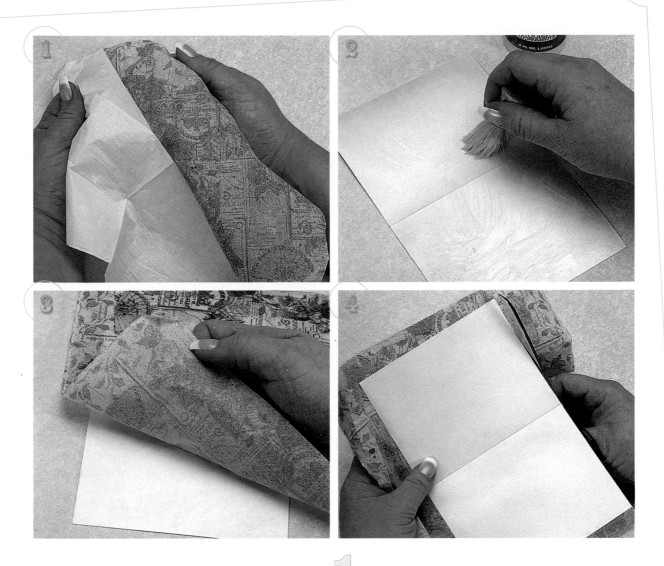

STEP ONE
Printed napkins are often two-ply. Carefully pull the printed layer from the plain backing.

STEP TWO
Brush an even layer of glue on the selected cardstock.

STEP THREE
Smooth the napkin onto the cardstock gently with a bone folder or ruler.

STEP FOUR
Trim away any excess napkin.

STEP FIVE

Fold the cardstock. Cut out flowers from old gift wrap and glue them on for extra decoration.

STEP SIX

Glue on an old playing card. Trim off any collage pieces hanging over the cardstock edges. Let dry.

STEP SEVEN

Choose the copy of the photo to be used inside the frame. Trace around the frame on the photo with a black permanent marker or pen.

STEP EIGHT

So that the color of the metal frame is better suited to the card, use a gold leafing pen over the metal rim. Set it aside to dry completely for about five minutes.

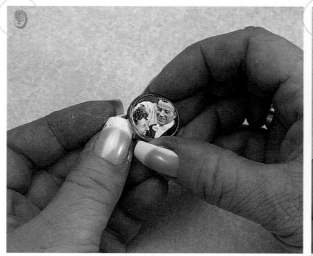

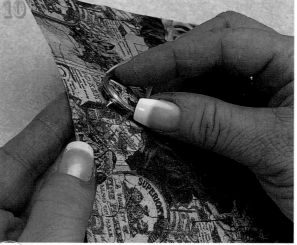

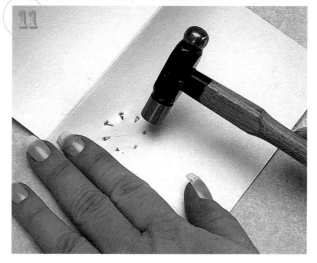

TIP

👉

FOR ADDED SHINE,

YOU CAN INSERT A

PIECE OF ACETATE OR

MICA BEFORE THE

PHOTO IS ADDED.

STEP NINE

Trim the photo on the inside of the marker or pen marking (from step 7) and insert the photo into the frame.

STEP TEN

Push the spikes through the cardstock.

STEP ELEVEN

Turn over the cardstock. With a small hammer, tack down the spikes. Tack them toward the center (inward) so that the frame will lay flat.

MATERIALS LIST
- page from old dictionary or book
- glue
- folded cardstock
- bone folder (or ruler)
- circle cutter (or punch or craft knife)
- 5" x 7" (13cm x 18cm) old school photo (or a color copy)
- gold foil embellishment

I know when I look through old leftover school photos, there are always a few big ones—photos that were meant to be framed and never quite made it! These larger pictures are perfect for a funny card that looks innocent from the outside and then becomes a giant retro shocker inside, especially if the clothes or hair in the picture are exceptionally dated. Have fun with this one.

CREATIVE MATERIALS:
old school photo, page from an old dictionary or book

< **SCHOOL DAYS** >

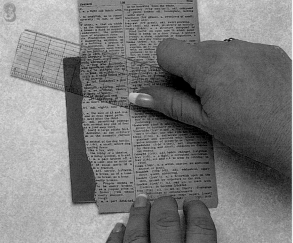

STEP ONE

Tear a page from an old dictionary or book.

STEP TWO

Spread glue over the front two-thirds of the cardstock.

STEP THREE

Attach the old page to the front of the cardstock, leaving the torn edge approximately ¾" (2cm) from the fold. Smooth the paper gently with a bone folder or a ruler.

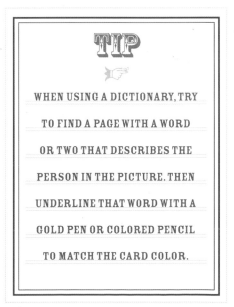

TIP

WHEN USING A DICTIONARY, TRY
TO FIND A PAGE WITH A WORD
OR TWO THAT DESCRIBES THE
PERSON IN THE PICTURE. THEN
UNDERLINE THAT WORD WITH A
GOLD PEN OR COLORED PENCIL
TO MATCH THE CARD COLOR.

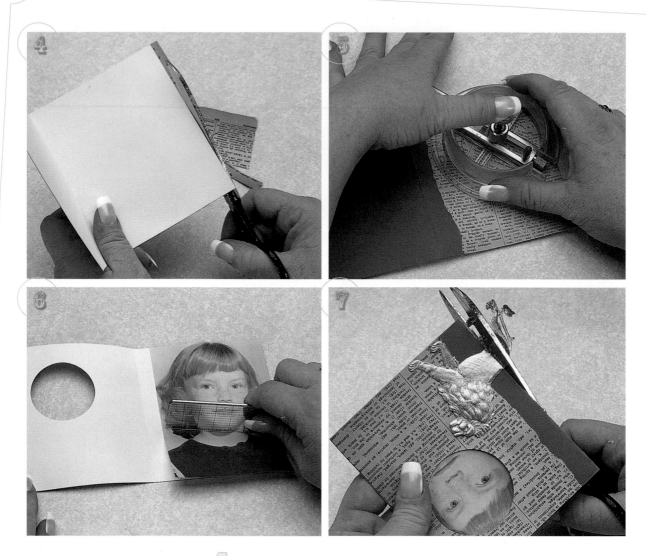

STEP FOUR
Trim away the excess.

STEP FIVE
Using a circle cutter, punch or craft knife, cut a circle (approximately 2¼" [6cm] in diameter) toward the top of the card .

STEP SIX
Choose a 5" x 7" (13cm x 18cm) color copy of an old school photo. Insert the copy into the card so that the face is positioned fully in the circular window. Glue the copy to the interior of the card, then smooth the card with the ruler.

STEP SEVEN
Add a few appropriate embellishments. Here I added a gold foil lion, since I am a Leo (yes, that's me, age six). Trim as needed.

Family Foray

Asymmetry can be very pleasing to the eye. Offsetting the circle picture window makes an otherwise sym-metrical card more interesting.

Several smaller circles of family or friends on a single card would make a unique card for the holidays or a reunion!

‹ CABOCHON CROWN ›

After creating several cards, my copies are generally in shreds. I usually have a few tiny faces left along with circle cutouts from other window cards. Here is a unique window card from those leftover scraps.

The cabochon is the perfect size for tiny faces and can be found at most craft and bead stores. I framed the cabochon with a rusty crown washer. I found the rusty crown washers at my local army surplus store! Needless to say I bought them all.

CREATIVE MATERIALS:
leftover scraps from other window cards, cabochon, crown washer

58

MATERIALS LIST
- Diamond Glaze
- color-copied photo
- clear acrylic cabochon
- leftover window card cutout
- folded cardstock
- doublestick tape
- crown washer
- copper tape

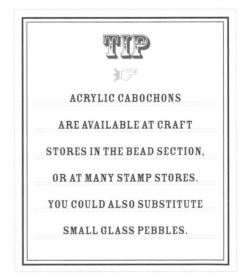

STEP ONE
Put a dab of Diamond Glaze on the picture.

STEP TWO
Drop the cabochon over the picture. Let the piece dry, then trim closely around the edge of the cabochon.

STEP THREE
Place the leftover cutout (this circle had a bit of a trim on one side) in the upper left corner of the cardstock with doublestick tape.

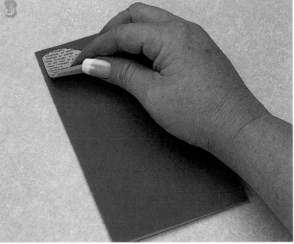

TIP

ACRYLIC CABOCHONS
ARE AVAILABLE AT CRAFT
STORES IN THE BEAD SECTION,
OR AT MANY STAMP STORES.
YOU COULD ALSO SUBSTITUTE
SMALL GLASS PEBBLES.

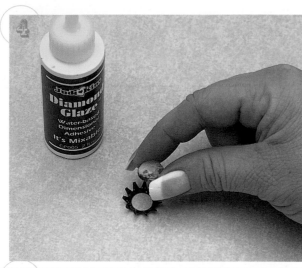

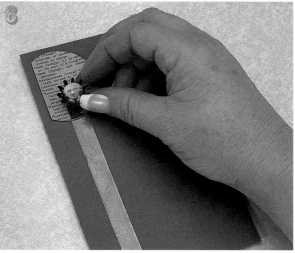

STEP FOUR

Apply a small amount of glue to the inside rim of the crown washer. Place the cabochon into the washer. Let dry.

STEP FIVE

Copper tape is a great accent on cards with metal embellishments. It is generally used for stained glass. The tape also comes in silver and brass. This tape has a release liner or backing piece that needs to be removed before applying it to the surface. To keep the tape from sticking to itself, attach just the top portion by pulling back the release liner. Then pull the liner slowly while positioning the tape onto the cardstock.

STEP SIX

Glue on the cabochon.

Family Jewel

With the ribbon and cabochon, you have the beginnings of a necklace. Simply add a jump ring to attach the cabochon to the ribbon, and you're ready to go.

Crown Jewel

A card that's a gift, too! This card's embellishment is a ready-made necklace. Remove the ribbon and attached cabochon, and use it as a choker necklace.

MATERIALS LIST

- beeswax
- color-copied photo
- disposable paintbrush
- cardstock
- craft knife
- heat gun
- old-fashioned design stamp
- gold, black or brown pigment or solvent inks
- gold leafing pen
- paper towels
- deep purple folded cardstock
- photo corners
- doublestick tape

TECHNIQUE:
Beeswax as Adhesive

I use only real beeswax for these techniques because it gives an antique look and is still transparent. It also remains easy to work with once it has cooled. And the best part about beeswax is the honey scent!

Beeswax is usually found at large craft stores or good art supply houses in the fabric paint aisle, or with the candle-making supplies.

I cannot emphasize this statement enough: Be extremely careful with hot wax! Not only can it be difficult to remove from surfaces—it can burn you! Needless to say, these are not projects I recommend for children.

< IMPRESSIONS *in* WAX >

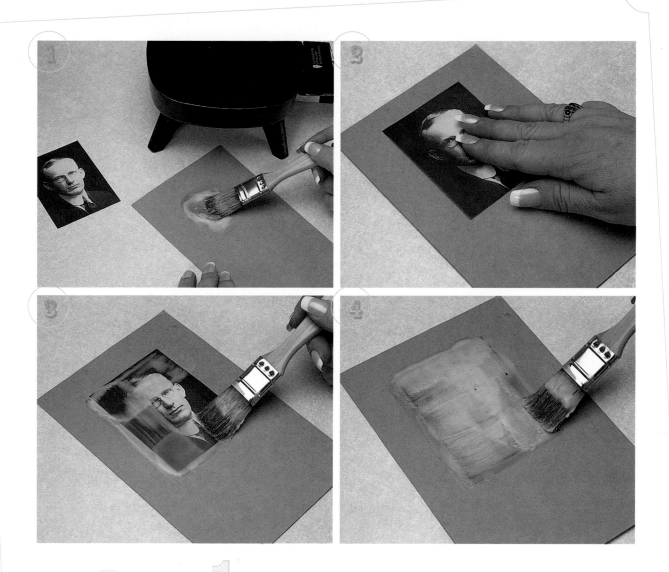

STEP ONE

Before you begin, find something to melt the wax in. The wax must remain hot while you are working on each piece, so you will want a heat source that has good temperature control. I prefer a small electric skillet. Heat the wax until it is clear but not boiling. Trim the copied photo. Use a cheap disposable paintbrush that does not shed too much to place a small amount of hot wax on the cardstock.

STEP TWO

Quickly place the picture on the wax to secure it in place.

STEP THREE

Evenly brush the wax over the photo.

STEP FOUR

Continue to brush layers of wax over the picture until you can barely see the image. Try to keep the edges as even as possible.

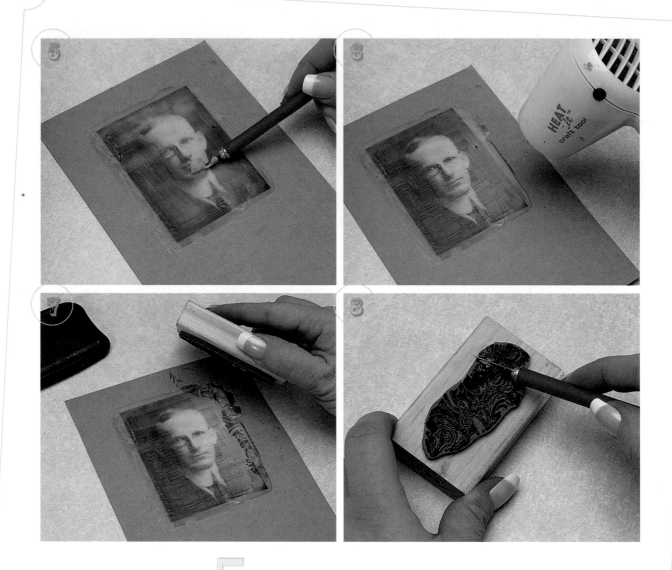

STEP FIVE

When the wax has set, carefully scrape through the wax to reveal the image, especially around the face. Leave the wax thicker on the edges of the piece. Add texture by scratching lines into the wax with a craft knife.

STEP SIX

On the thick edges, soften the wax with a heat gun. Just a little heat to soften—do not remelt the wax.

STEP SEVEN

Stamp old-fashioned designs into the edges of the wax. Pigment or solvent inks work best on wax. Gold, black or brown inks look nice on the yellowish wax.

STEP EIGHT

If wax becomes embedded in the stamp, scrape it off with a craft knife. Then apply a little heat with the heat gun and wipe quickly with a paper towel.

TIP

USE WAX PAPER AND
TWINE TO WRAP THE
CARD FOR A VINTAGE
LOOK. WHEN MAILING
CARDS LIKE THIS, A
SMALL, THIN (JEWELRY)
BOX IS PREFERABLE TO
AN ENVELOPE.

STEP NINE
Scrape and scratch the card surface again for texture.

STEP TEN
Trim the cardstock evenly around the waxed area. Repeat the same stamped image in soft brown around the edge of the cardstock.

STEP ELEVEN
Edge the cardstock with a gold leafing pen.

STEP TWELVE
Affix the finished piece to the deep purple cardstock using photo corners and a small piece of doublestick tape.

< KID STUFF >

This picture is of my Uncle Jack and his friends. On this card, instead of glitter, I used small mica chips. They have a much more antiqued look than other glitters available today and are easily adhered with wax or glue.

TECHNIQUE:
Beeswax as Adhesive

CREATIVE MATERIALS:
mica tile, mica chips, old buttons

66

MATERIALS LIST
- beeswax
- color-copied photo
- heavy cardstock
- brush
- large mica tile
- mica chips
- gold foil letters
- heat gun
- craft knife
- old buttons
- gold leafing pen
- folded cardstock
- doublestick tape
- ribbon

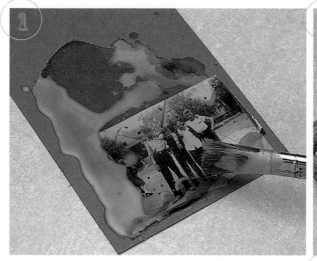

STEP ONE

Melt the wax as described on page 63. Trim the copy of a photo. Secure the picture to heavy cardstock by brushing on a small amount of wax. Layer a large mica tile over the picture, then add wax around the edges to hold it in place.

STEP TWO

Build up the wax around the edges by drizzling it from the brush. While the wax is still hot, add mica chips. Cover the chips with more wax.

STEP THREE

Add a layer of wax at the top of the picture, then quickly apply gold foil letters.

CAUTION

HOT WAX CAN CAUSE BURNS. BE CAUTIOUS WHEN USING.

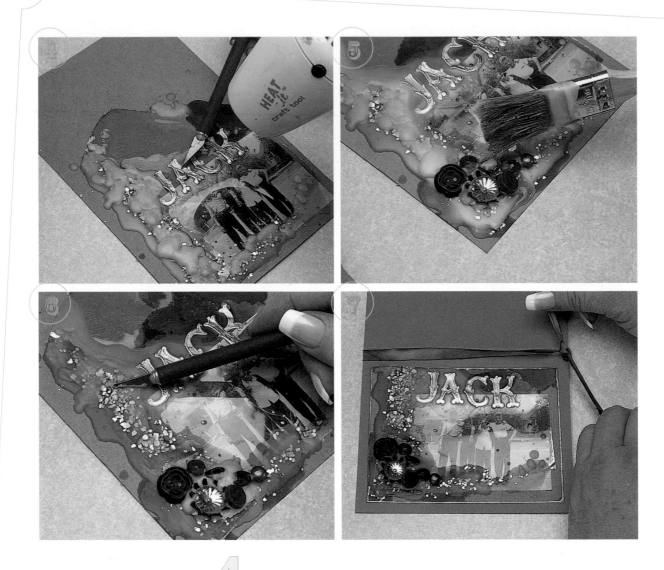

STEP FOUR
Warm the wax with a heat gun, then adjust the letters with the tip of a craft knife.

STEP FIVE
Reheat the wax and add old buttons. Drip wax over the buttons to secure them.

STEP SIX
Let the piece set up. Then scrape away selected areas to reveal more of the chips, buttons and foil letters.

STEP SEVEN
Trim the cardstock, then edge it with a gold leafing pen. Adhere to the folded cardstock with doublestick tape. Accent the card with a ribbon.

Party Time

The background piece is terra–cotta paper dipped in beeswax. The beeswax turned the paper a darker color. Test all papers beforehand, so you don't have any color surprises.

Snowy Day

The background paper was antiqued using repeated light washes of walnut ink. The entire band—background paper, foil frame and photo—was dipped in beeswax.

‹ VINTAGE SANTA ›

This great old photo shows my mother and her twin brother visiting the scariest Santa I have ever seen. The original photo is faint, so I have copied it in a darker tone and given it an eight percent color screen. Color copies for this technique must be carbon-based toner copies, not laser printed. Select a photo that has high contrast: all-light or all-dark photos will not transfer clearly. The perfect photo has very definite lights and darks in the same picture. Many glues or gel mediums and pigment powders will work for this technique.

TECHNIQUE:
Gel Photo Transfer

CREATIVE MATERIAL:
mica pieces

MATERIALS LIST

- Omni Gel
- color-copied photo (made with carbon-based toner)
- brush
- ceramic tile (or other slick surface)
- mica
- Diamond Glaze
- rusty brown Piñata Color (alcohol ink)
- hole punch
- white and dark cardstock
- small brads
- small flat beads
- doublestick tape
- folded cardstock

STEP ONE
Place a large dollop of Omni Gel on the copied photo.

STEP TWO
Brush the glue horizontally. Let the glue set for a minute.

STEP THREE
Add another dollop of Omni Gel and brush it vertically over the copy. Repeat the process several times, brushing diagonally, vertically and horizontally. Let the piece dry overnight.

STEP FOUR
Trim away the excess copy paper.

STEP FIVE
Submerge the piece in water. When paper is wet enough, it will look very mottled.

STEP SIX
To remove the paper, place the piece glue-side-down on a tile or other slick surface, to keep it from slipping and tearing the transfer.

STEP SEVEN
Rub the paper off of the transfer with your fingers, keeping the surface wet.

STEP EIGHT
Cut the mica to fit the photo transfer.

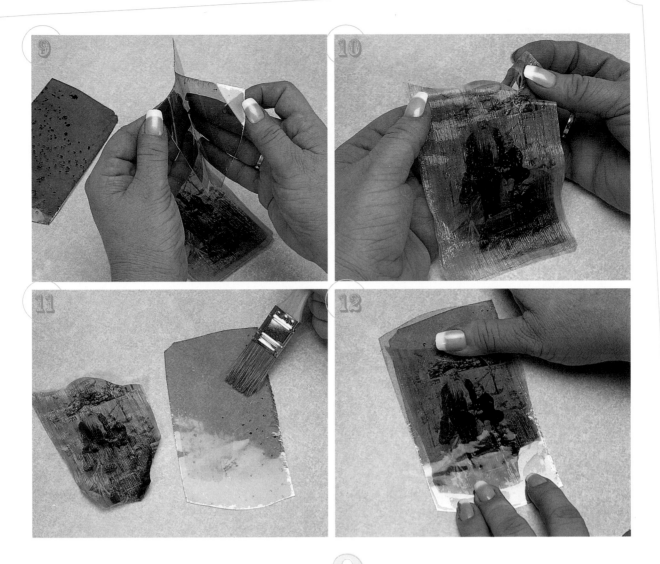

STEP NINE
Separate the mica piece into thin sheets.

STEP TEN
Carefully tear the gel transfer to give it a raw edge.

STEP ELEVEN
Apply Diamond Glaze to the mica.

STEP TWELVE
Position the gel transfer faceup on top of the mica. Add a little Diamond Glaze to the front corners of the transfer, then layer another piece of mica on top of the transfer.

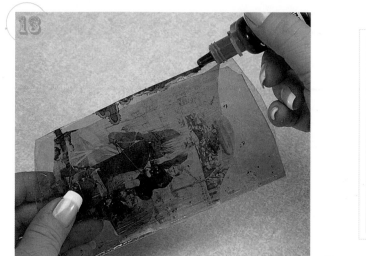

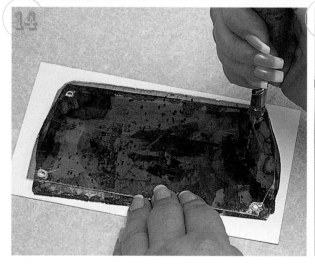

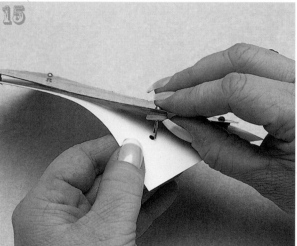

STEP THIRTEEN

Drip a little rusty brown Piñata Color onto the mica edges to give the mica an aged look.

STEP FOURTEEN

Punch holes through the mica and the white cardstock.

STEP FIFTEEN

Attach the mica to the white cardstock using small brads through the punched holes. Add small flat beads to act as separators. This little bit of spacing allows light in behind the mica. Attach the white cardstock to dark cardstock using doublestick tape. Then attach the dark cardstock layer to the front of folded cardstock using doublestick tape.

Treasures

Here I used the liquid transfer method, but did not remove all of the paper. For photos without good contrast, leave some of the paper so the image shows through better.

Happy Heart

After I transferred the image for this card, I dipped it and the mica into beeswax to give the image a leafy appearance. I embellished the card using common charms that can be found in most craft stores.

MATERIALS LIST

- rubber stamp
- mica tile
- black solvent ink
- red Piñata Color (alcohol ink)
- brush
- spray water bottle
- cardstock
- walnut ink
- Diamond Glaze
- game piece
- folded cardstock
- foil paper frame
- foil paper photo corners
- doublestick tape

Stamps can be used on a number of surfaces, not just cardstock. Here I've stamped an image onto a mica tile, using black solvent ink. Solvent inks work on almost every surface including paper, metal and wood, and they are exceptionally good on non-porous surfaces like plastics and mica. Solvent inks stay true and dry quickly making it easy to apply them to the finished piece.

TECHNIQUE:
Stamped Mica

CREATIVE MATERIALS:
mica tile, game piece, foil frame

⟨ **QUEEN T** ⟩

STEP ONE
Stamp an image directly onto the mica tile with a solvent black ink.

STEP TWO
Add four drops of red Piñata Color to the back of the tile.

STEP THREE
Use a brush to move the ink over the tile. Let dry.

STEP FOUR
Wet the edges of the cardstock, then apply walnut ink to the edges with a brush.

STEP FIVE

With a small amount of glue, attach the dry mica to the card-stock. Glue the game piece to the bottom right-hand corner. Using a brush, apply glue to the back of the foil paper frame.

STEP SIX

Attach the frame to the mica and press to secure.

STEP SEVEN

Trim the foil paper photo corners.

STEP EIGHT

Affix the cardstock piece to the folded cardstock using double-stick tape. Glue on the corners.

Solemn David

You don't need old photographs to make a vintage greeting card. This image was stamped onto mica using black solvent permanent ink. The background was stamped with a pigment pad and rubbed with shoe polish. The background was edged with a gold leafing pen.

Vision

These background leaves were stamped with dye and pigment inks and rubbed with brown shoe polish. I added a torn strip of vellum, before stamping the image onto mica.

Shipping tags are very versatile and can be used for more than just a tag. Here I've used the shipping tag as the main embellishment for the card.

I've made a variation of a transfer by changing the color and texture of the Omni Gel with pigment powder to create a tintype appearance. Any metallic color can be used to get this look.

TECHNIQUE:
Faux Tintype

CREATIVE MATERIALS:
shipping tag, mica chips, old ribbon

MATERIALS LIST

- walnut ink
- large shipping tag
- color-copied photo (made with carbon-based toner)
- scrap paper
- Omni Gel
- stiff brush
- metallic pigment powder
- paper towels
- mica chips
- glitter
- rubber stamp with word design
- black permanent ink
- old ribbon
- doublestick tape
- folded cardstock

STEP ONE

Apply a medium brown mixture of walnut ink to a large shipping tag (see pages 25–26 for information on mixing different ink strengths). Set aside to dry.

STEP TWO

Select a color copy to transfer. Trim the copy to the final size you want to apply to the tag. Lay the copy on scrap paper, picture side up. Apply a good dollop of Omni Gel to the copy. Dip a stiff brush into metallic pigment powder, then apply the powder to the wet glue.

STEP THREE

Brush on this mixture horizontally first. Wait a few seconds, then brush vertically. This mixture should be rather thick and even on the copy. Let it dry, then trim away the excess paper.

STEP FOUR

Soak the piece in water. Depending on the thickness of the copy and scrap paper, this could take a few minutes.

STEP FIVE
Peel the scrap paper away. Dip the piece back in the water. Gently begin rubbing the copy paper off of the metallic surface. Repeat this process until the paper has been removed. Blot dry with a paper towel.

STEP SIX
Adhere the tintype to the shipping tag by brushing a thin layer of glue onto the back of the tintype.

STEP SEVEN
Add a little glue around the edge of the tintype, then sprinkle on the mica chips and glitter.

STEP EIGHT
Ink your stamp with black permanent ink.

STEP NINE
Stamp the top of the tag with a large word pattern in black ink.

STEP TEN
Attach an old ribbon loop.

STEP ELEVEN
Using doublestick tape, apply the tag to folded cardstock.

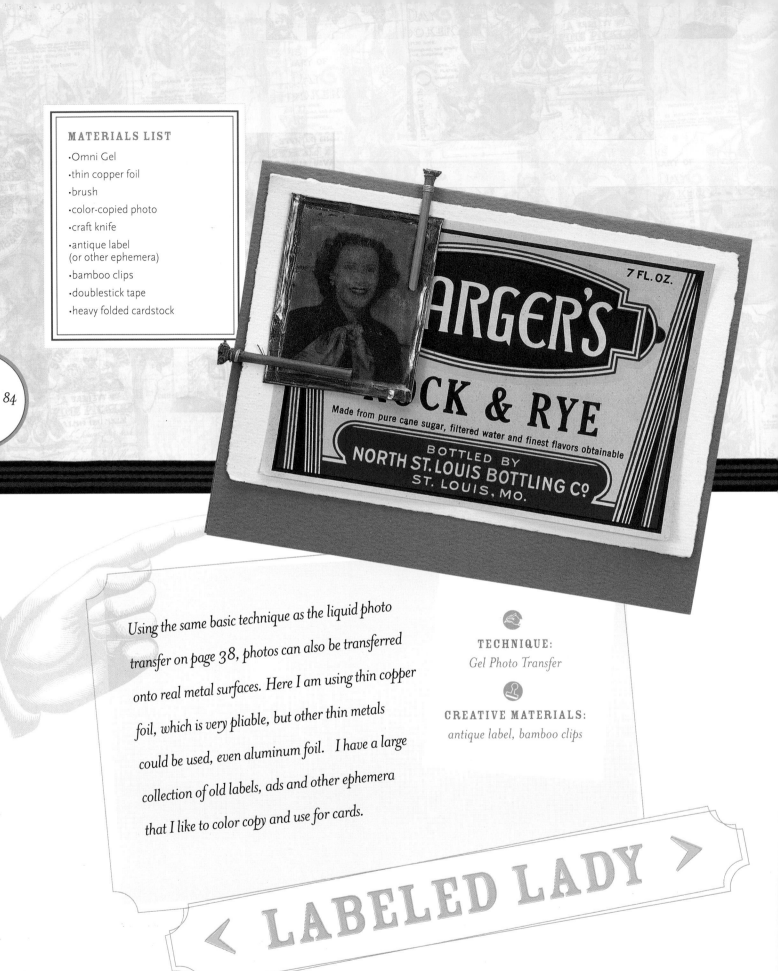

MATERIALS LIST

- Omni Gel
- thin copper foil
- brush
- color-copied photo
- craft knife
- antique label
  (or other ephemera)
- bamboo clips
- doublestick tape
- heavy folded cardstock

7 FL. OZ.

ARGER'S

OCK & RYE

Made from pure cane sugar, filtered water and finest flavors obtainable

BOTTLED BY
NORTH ST. LOUIS BOTTLING C^o
ST. LOUIS, MO.

Using the same basic technique as the liquid photo transfer on page 38, photos can also be transferred onto real metal surfaces. Here I am using thin copper foil, which is very pliable, but other thin metals could be used, even aluminum foil. I have a large collection of old labels, ads and other ephemera that I like to color copy and use for cards.

TECHNIQUE:
Gel Photo Transfer

CREATIVE MATERIALS:
antique label, bamboo clips

< LABELED LADY >

STEP ONE
Apply Omni Gel to a piece of foil (approximately a 2½" x 2⅛" [6cm x 5cm] piece), brushing horizontally. Cover the entire piece of foil. Then repeat the process with vertical strokes.

STEP TWO
Adhere the color copy face down to the gel.

STEP THREE
While the gel is still wet, remove the excess from the edges of the metal using a craft knife. Let dry.

STEP FOUR
Dip the piece in water to wet the paper. When the paper is wet through, it will have a mottled appearance. Begin rubbing the paper off of the metal. Repeat the process until the image can be seen and all of the paper has been removed.

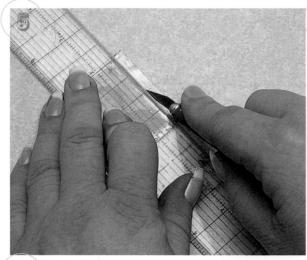

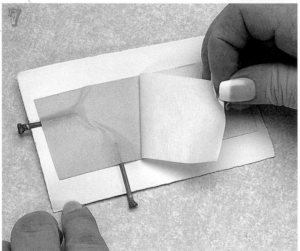

STEP FIVE

*To create a more finished edge on the metal, score ¼"
(6mm) inside all four sides with the back of a craft
knife. Turn under the edges.*

STEP SIX

*Attach the metal to an antique label or other ephemera
using bamboo clips.*

STEP SEVEN

*Secure the clips with a large piece of doublestick tape.
Add this piece to heavy folded cardstock.*

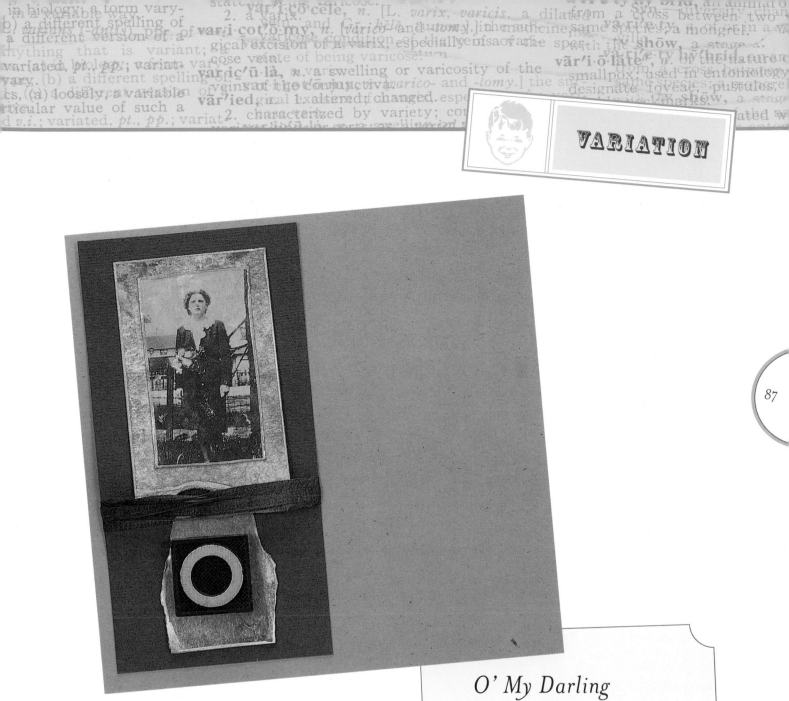

O' My Darling

To create a vintage look, use cotton, silk and wool ribbons rather than modern synthetic materials.

< RED RIDING HOOD >

The folds here are scored with the back of a craft knife. I like this type of scoring because it gives a very crisp crease. To achieve a more textured appearance, I like to crunch the metal then flatten it again, giving it an older look. The addition of the photo corners frames the metal and gives it a more finished appearance.

TECHNIQUE:
Stamped Metal

88

MATERIALS LIST

- metal piece
- scissors
- rubber stamp
- black solvent ink
- photo corners
- craft knife (or scoring tool)
- cardstock
- doublestick tape
- solid head eyelets
- hole punch
- eyelet setter
- hammer

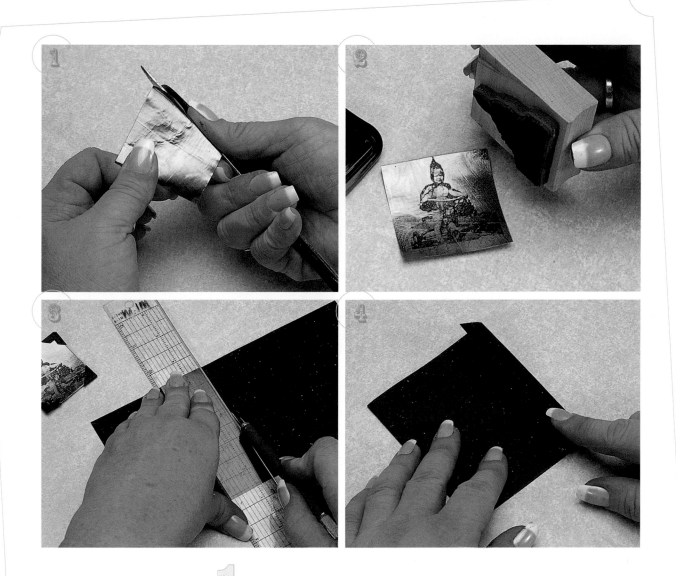

STEP ONE

This metal has a few crinkles in it. If yours does, too, run it along the back of a pair of scissors to smooth it out.

STEP TWO

Cut the metal to size. This piece is approximately 2" x 2" (5cm x 5cm). Stamp an image on the metal using black solvent ink. Add photo corners to the piece.

STEP THREE

Using a craft knife, score the cardstock 4" (10cm) in from the edge. Fold it over, then score again at the open edge. This creates a flap that is folded over the front of the card.

STEP FOUR

Fold over the flap.

STEP FIVE
Attach the stamped metal piece to the cardstock with doublestick tape.

STEP SIX
To make a metal band for the flap using leftover metal strips, attach equal widths of strips together with solid head eyelets. These eyelets work in the same fashion as regular eyelets; they simply have a solid head on the top. Punch ⅛" (3mm) holes on each end of the strips.

STEP SEVEN
Insert the first solid head into a punched hole. Then turn over the piece and hammer the eyelet back down. Wrap the strip around the card flap to adjust the fit. Remove the strip from the card and insert the final eyelet. Set it with the hammer.

STEP EIGHT
The band should slide right on over the flap.

Babycakes

For a different look, I used solid head eyelets to attach the metal picture. Solid head eyelets are a one-piece snap, and they work the same way as regular eyelets (see Resources on page 126).

Baby Face

To achieve the multiple colors in the metal, I sporadically heated the metal sheet with a barbecue lighter. The heat transforms a copper-colored sheet of metal into a rainbow of colors.

MATERIALS LIST

- rusted metal corners
- metal clippers
- sharp craft knife
- postcard with flower design
- color-copied photo booth photo
- scoring tool
- cardstock
- doublestick tape
- glue
- vintage ribbon

Good friend.
busy tho' I be,
I have yet
a thought
for thee.

G380

Pictures from photo booths are not so easy to find in antique stores any— more. Luckily I have a few of my own. Some of the expressions are priceless. They are beautifully paired with old postcards, which are still widely available and relatively inexpensive. Many of the old postcards have lovely sentiments, and the size of these photos are easily worked into the design of a card using a simple slot.

CREATIVE MATERIALS:
photo booth picture, old ribbon,
vintage postcard

< FOREVER FRIENDS >

STEP ONE
I have chosen to use rusted metal corners, available at many craft stores, for this project. These corners are quite large, so I am using some small metal clippers to cut them in half.

STEP TWO
With a sharp new craft knife, cut around part of the postcard design. Even though this flower design is complicated to cut around, the size of the opening needed for the photo is fairly small.

STEP THREE
Cut out one photo booth copy. Insert the copy into the slot in the postcard.

STEP FOUR
Score and fold the cardstock.

STEP FIVE

Apply doublestick tape to the back of the postcard. Cover the corner of the copy with tape as well. Attach the piece to the greeting card.

STEP SIX

Add a dot of glue to the corners of the postcard. Spread the glue a bit with the craft knife. Lay the rusted metal corners on the glue.

STEP SEVEN

Toward the bottom of the card, create a band by tying on a vintage ribbon.

TIP

USING BANDS THAT NEED TO BE REMOVED ADD TO THE ANTICIPATION OF OPENING THE CARD! IT MAKES A SIMPLE CARD SEEM MORE LIKE A PRESENT.

Old Money

The circle punch fit perfectly into the circle on the colonial money to provide a picture window. Reproduction colonial money is available from many East Coast historical societies.

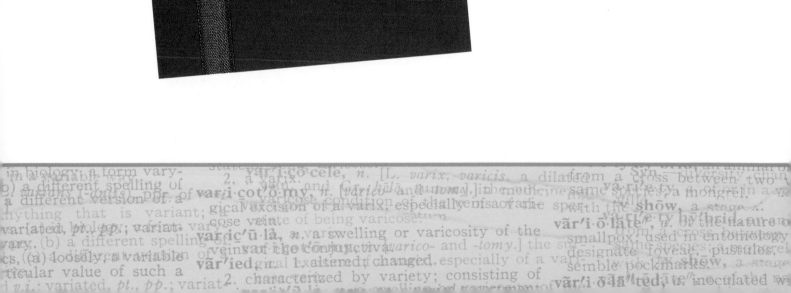

< TRIPLICATE >

By using a thick application of watercolor paint over stamped images then removing a small bit of the paint by adding water and blotting, you can create a wonderful faux fresco that has the feel of paint peeling away revealing hidden pictures. Use only inexpensive or student–grade watercolors for this project. Good water–colors are too expensive for this project.

TECHNIQUE:
Faux Fresco

CREATIVE MATERIAL:
vintage jewels

MATERIALS LIST
- rubber stamp
- black solvent ink
- watercolor paper
- tube watercolor paints
- stiff brush
- heat gun
- paintbrush (or watercolor brush)
- paper towel
- iridescent pigment ink
- folded cardstock
- doublestick tape
- vintage jewels
- clear glue

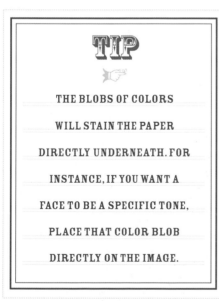

TIP

THE BLOBS OF COLORS
WILL STAIN THE PAPER
DIRECTLY UNDERNEATH. FOR
INSTANCE, IF YOU WANT A
FACE TO BE A SPECIFIC TONE,
PLACE THAT COLOR BLOB
DIRECTLY ON THE IMAGE.

STEP ONE
Stamp an image three times with black solvent ink onto water–color paper.

STEP TWO
Place small blobs of watercolor paint over the stamped images.

STEP THREE
Using a stiff brush, dab the paint over the images, completely covering them. Try not to overmix the colors.

STEP FOUR
Let dry or use a heat gun to speed the drying.

STEP FIVE

With a paintbrush, apply a little puddle of water where the image was.

STEP SIX

Blot the water away by pressing with a paper towel for a few seconds. Do not pat the water off. Patting will blend the paint.

STEP SEVEN

Repeat the process until parts of the images can be seen.

STEP EIGHT

Trim away the excess paper. For further decoration, add a few designs on the edges with iridescent pigment ink.

STEP NINE

Mount the piece on cardstock using doublestick tape. Add a few vintage jewels with a tiny amount of glue.

Porcelain Fresco

*Use a light touch when removing paint.
You want to make sure you have a good
light/dark contrast and a nice balance of
the matte and watercolor finishes.*

Triplets

*Photo corners are a quick and easy
way to attach a layer of paper.
And these lick-and-stick photo
corners are especially easy because
you don't need glue or tape.*

MATERIALS LIST

- cardstock
- tube watercolor paints, light and dark
- brush
- heat gun
- design stamp
- folded cardstock
- doublestick tape
- copied photo
- photo corners

Using watercolor paint without added water can create a very textured look and feel to plain paper. The texture makes this card background look like antique wallpaper. If you like a more shimmery look, use a light metallic pigment ink instead of watercolor.

TECHNIQUE:
Faux Wallpaper

< PORTRAIT >

STEP ONE

*Place globs of dark watercolor paint all over a piece of
cardstock. Use a pouncing motion with your brush to move
the paint.*

STEP TWO

Let dry, or speed up the drying time with a heat gun.

STEP THREE

Apply light watercolor paint to the design stamp using a brush.

TIP

THIS IS A GREAT

TECHNIQUE FOR GRUNGY

OR DISCOLORED PAPERS.

THE PAINT COVERS

EVERYTHING, EVEN

EMBOSSED SURFACES.

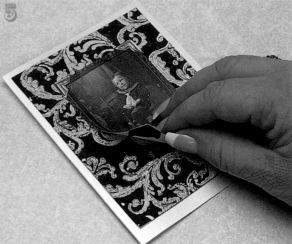

STEP FOUR

Stamp the image on the painted piece. Stamp the design off the edges, turning the paper as you go.

STEP FIVE

Trim down the cardstock to fit the front of the folded cardstock and mount it with doublestick tape. Trim a copied picture to fit and attach with photo corners.

TIP

WHEN CHOOSING THE COLORS OF PAINT,
REMEMBER THAT THE HIGHER THE CONTRAST,
THE MORE INTERESTING THE BACKGROUND
WILL BE. IF THE BACKGROUND NEEDS TO BE
MORE SUBTLE, A MONOCHROMATIC LOOK
WOULD BE A GREAT WAY TO GO.

Three Monkeys

Use decorative scissors to create an interesting border that sets off the different layers.

Family Ties

For different effects, try the faux wallpaper technique on various paper finishes. I used a shimmer, coated paper for the yellow layer.

< MIRROR IMAGE >

Flat surfaces don't have to look flat. Use layers of textures to achieve dimension. I colored a small mirror with alcohol inks, added a stamped design and finished it by applying a cutout photo collaged to the front. This piece can also be made into a fun necklace. Layer the mirror onto or place it inside of an old watch case or locket.

104

TECHNIQUE:
Stamped Mirror

CREATIVE MATERIALS:
small mirror, ribbon

MATERIALS LIST

- assorted Piñata Colors (alcohol inks)
- small round mirror
- paper towels
- Claro Extender
- rubber stamp
- watercolor paint
- color-copied photo
- Diamond Glaze
- paintbrush
- gold leafing pen
- folded cardstock
- ribbon
- clear glue

STEP ONE

Apply a few drops of yellow Piñata Color to the mirror. Allow the ink to spread.

STEP TWO

Add a couple drops of other colors until there is a nice mix of colors. Let dry.

STEP THREE

If the ink becomes too dark or muddy, blot gently with a paper towel, then add a drop or two of Claro Extender.

STEP FOUR

Stamp a design with watercolor paint on the mirror.

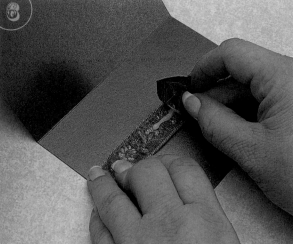

STEP FIVE

Cut out a copied image. Trim the image so it fits right along the mirror edge. Spread a thin layer of Diamond Glaze over the mirror. Lay the cutout on the mirror. If you want the cutout to be glossy, spread a small amount of Diamond Glaze over the image. Let dry. Edge the mirror with a gold leafing pen.

STEP SIX

Attach ribbon around the front of the card vertically. Glue the ribbon ends together inside the card.

STEP SEVEN

On the front of the card, glue the mirror to the center of the ribbon.

New World

To apply an image onto the mirror after it has been painted, let it dry thoroughly. Then stamp the image onto the mirror using black solvent ink.

Setting Sun

To create a mottled look on the mirror, dab off some of the wet ink with a paper towel. This lets more of the mirror show through.

MATERIALS LIST

- white or light color polymer clay
- pasta machine or acrylic clay roller
- tissue blade
- color-copied dark photo
- rolling pin
- craft knife or sharp scissors
- gold leafing pen
- page from an old book
- Omni Gel (or Diamond Glaze)
- folded cardstock
- doublestick tape
- vintage ribbon
- pearl-headed pin
- wire cutters
- game piece (or button)

Polymer clay is a great medium for greeting cards; it is lightweight, can be rolled flat and is perfect for transferring photos. I prefer Premo! clay because it remains a little flexible when dry, which is excellent for greeting cards. Use utensils kept especially for polymer clay. If you don't want to invest in a pasta machine, an acrylic clay roller is available at most craft stores.

TECHNIQUE:
Polymer Clay Photo Transfer

CREATIVE MATERIALS:
page from old book, vintage ribbon, game piece

< HERITAGE CLAY >

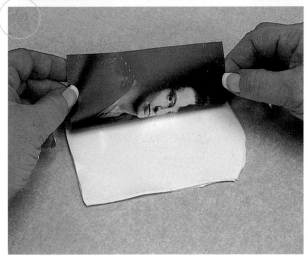

1 STEP ONE

Using white or a very light color of polymer clay, condition the clay by running it through a pasta machine. This process is simple. Begin by flattening one end of a block of clay. Feed the flat end into the rollers, then continue rolling until all of the clay is through.

2 STEP TWO

Cut the clay in half with a tissue blade. Lay one piece on top of the other, then roll through the machine again. Repeat this process several times until the clay has no visible air pockets and is soft.

3 STEP THREE

Change the machine to the widest setting. Cut and stack the clay as in step two, then trim away the excess clay to create a rectangle. Run this through the machine.

4 STEP FOUR

Select and trim a color copy of a very dark photo. The most intense photos turn out best. Cut the clay to the size of the photo. Lay the copy of the photo face down on the clay.

STEP FIVE

Roll over the photo with a rolling pin or acrylic roller to adhere it to the clay. Bake the clay according to the package directions.

STEP SIX

Remove the clay from the oven. Immediately roll again with the rolling pin. Slowly peel off the copy paper. Let cool for five minutes, then flip the clay over and cool for another five minutes. This prevents the thin clay from curling.

STEP SEVEN

Trim the clay with sharp scissors or a craft knife.

STEP EIGHT

Use a gold leafing pen to color the edge of the clay.

STEP NINE

Tear a page from an old book. Glue the page to the front of the folded card-stock. Trim away the excess.

STEP TEN

Use glue or doublestick tape to adhere the clay to the front of the card.

STEP ELEVEN

Create a small fan with a piece of vintage ribbon and secure it with a pearl-headed pin. Snip off the sharp end of the pin with wire cutters.

STEP TWELVE

Glue the fan to the cardstock, tucking it slightly under the clay photo.

STEP THIRTEEN

Attach a game piece or button with a little glue.

< REMEMBER >

Make an old–fashioned frame for photos by using a translucent polymer clay. Translucent clay is the best to start with if you are a beginner because it is easy to tell when the clay is fully baked. When completely baked, this clay has a yellowish, alabaster look and will be slightly blotchy.

TECHNIQUE:
Polymer Clay Frames

MATERIALS LIST

- color-copied photos made with carbon-based toner
- translucent polymer clay
- pasta machine or acrylic clay roller
- craft knife
- nail file
- gold leafing pen
- copper ink
- rubber stamp
- heat gun
- clear glue
- folded cardstock
- doublestick tape

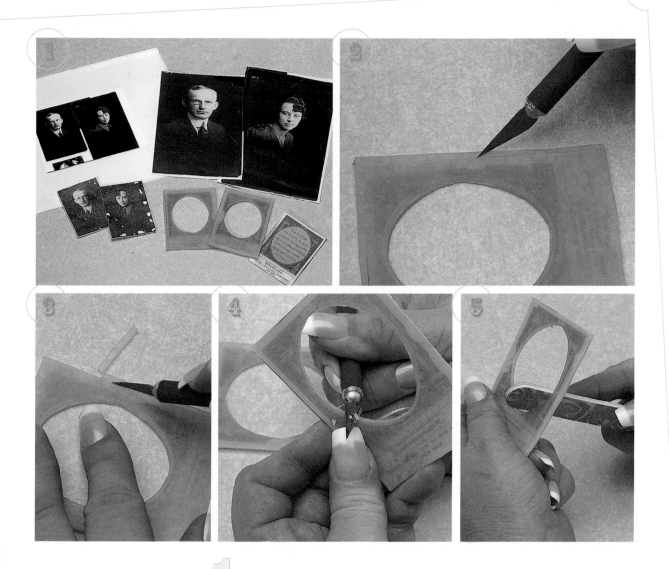

STEP ONE

Select and size the images to be transferred. The photocopies must be done on a copying machine using carbon-based toner. Transfer the photo images onto white clay and the frame images onto translucent clay, as described on pages 109 and 110.

STEP TWO

Cut out the frames after baking by carefully scoring around the inside oval. Cut through the clay slowly, then score the outside edges.

STEP THREE

Trim the clay edges using a craft knife.

STEP FOUR

Smooth out any rough edges with a craft knife by carefully shaving the clay.

STEP FIVE

Sand the edges with a nail file.

STEP SIX

Color the inside and outside edges of the frame with the gold leafing pen.

STEP SEVEN

Stamp a word or decoration on the frame with copper ink. Dry the ink with a heat gun.

STEP EIGHT

Put glue on the corners of the photo pieces, then position the frame over them. Let dry.

STEP NINE

Attach the frames to folded cardstock with doublestick tape.

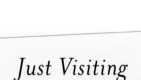

All in the Family

To get a more finished, professional-looking edge around the polymer clay transfers, coat the edges with paint or a colored pen.

Just Visiting

Mica works great as a background as well as an overlay, as seen in Vintage Santa on page 70.

MATERIALS LIST

- light molding paste
- liquid acrylic (or ink)
- rubber stamp or image
- heavy cardstock
- buttons in various sizes
- tiny jewels
- mica chips
- spray water bottle
- brush
- walnut ink
- folded cardstock
- doublestick tape
- black rickrack

Molding paste is a fun compound that can be textured with sand, beads, buttons, mica and more. The light version is awesome for greeting cards, since it is extremely lightweight.

Molding paste can be colored with a variety of products including inks, powdered pigment and acrylics. I prefer Golden Fluid Acrylics. They are so intensely pigmented that a little goes a long way.

TECHNIQUE:
Walnut Ink

CREATIVE MATERIALS:
molding paste, buttons, mica chips, tiny jewels, rickrack

< TEXTURED PAST >

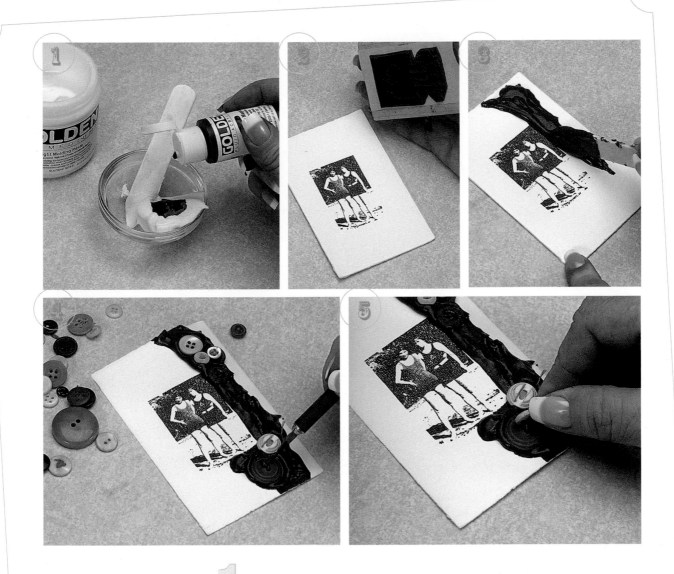

STEP ONE

Mix a couple of generous tablespoons of light molding paste with several drops of liquid acrylic or ink until you have achieved the desired color. Set aside.

STEP TWO

Stamp or photocopy an image onto heavy cardstock.

STEP THREE

Spread the molding paste along one side of the cardstock.

STEP FOUR

Apply the largest and most colorful button first. Press it firmly into the paste so the button holes fill with the paste.

STEP FIVE

Layer smaller buttons over the paste, making sure each button has enough paste for a secure bond.

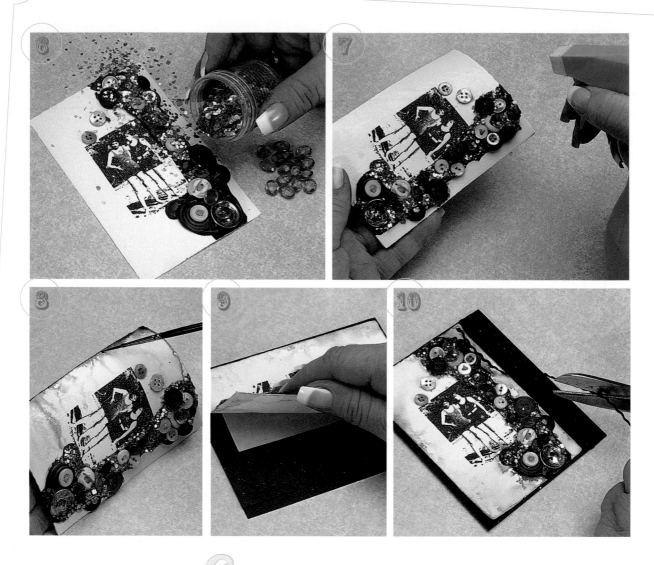

STEP SIX
Place tiny jewels and sprinkle mica chips over the surface. Let dry for thirty minutes.

STEP SEVEN
Spritz the other half of the cardstock with water.

STEP EIGHT
Brush a small amount of walnut ink onto the edge of the cardstock. Let dry.

STEP NINE
Attach the piece to the folded cardstock with doublestick tape.

STEP TEN
Tie on a skinny piece of black rickrack.

Bead and Button

Be sure to use light molding paste on greeting cards. Regular molding paste is heavier and will need additional postage to mail. It will also take longer to dry.

Sisters

When using complicated embellishments, keep the main image simple so the card doesn't look too busy or over-designed.

Window to Holland

The photo used in this card is a picture of my grandmother in Holland, before she and her family moved to America. I used a typewriter key ring to frame the definition of portrait. Typewriter key rings are available from Coffee Break Design (see Resources on page 126 for information).

☞ **CREATIVE MATERIALS:**
vintage napkin and typewriter key ring

Faith

Use the faux wallpaper technique on white paper. Paint the lips and eyes using colors from the wallpaper.

☞ **TECHNIQUE:**
Faux Wallpaper

120

Wild West

Instead of polishing the polymer clay, I applied a layer of Diamond Glaze over the clay to create a nice sheen.

☞ **TECHNIQUE:**
Polymer Clay Photo Transfer

American Gothic

Instead of transferring a photograph onto metal, transfer the photo onto pearlized paper to achieve a metallic look.

☞ **TECHNIQUE:**
Liquid Photo Transfer

First Love

For embellishment, I used photographic stickers (stickers made from actual photos; available at craft stores). I stained them with shoe polish to make them darker and more vintage in appearance.

☞ TECHNIQUE:
Liquid Photo Transfer

Beautiful View

Spread on a thin layer of molding paste with a palette knife or credit card. The background was antiqued using walnut ink.

☞ TECHNIQUE:
Walnut Ink

Love in Bloom

Use shoe polish to age the greeting card roses for a more vintage look.

☞ **TECHNIQUE:**
Shoe Polish Overlay

Through the Keyhole

To create a sea glass look, I filled a rubber washer (or o-ring) with Diamond Glaze.

☞ **TECHNIQUE:**
Faux Fresco

A is for Arthur

Instead of gluing the game piece, I adhered it with beeswax.

☞ **TECHNIQUE:**

Beeswax as Adhesive

That's My Chicken

Don't throw away leftover scraps because you never know when they might fit perfectly onto another card. The circle piece used here is the leftover cutout from the colonial money used in Old Money on page 95.

☞ **CREATIVE MATERIAL:**

sea glass

Food for Thought

To visually unify the third layer of the card, I dipped the mica pieces and the gems in beeswax.

☞ **TECHNIQUE:**
Beeswax as Adhesive

Attic Baby

To change the color of the molding paste, I used Piñata Colors after it was dry.

☞ **CREATIVE MATERIALS:**
molding paste and buttons

RESOURCES

❧☞ WALNUT INK GRANULES, WORD SLAB STAMPS, STAMPS

Postmodern Design
P.O. Box 720416
Norman, OK 73070
(405) 321-3176
(405) 321-2296 fax
email: postmoderndesign@aol.com

< ♘ > *Stamps used on pages 2, 8, 20, 38, 43, 112, 120*

❧☞ LIQUID WALNUT INK, STAMPS

Stampers Anonymous
Williamsburg Square
25967 Detroit Rd.
Westlake, OH 44145
(440) 250-9112 or (888) 326-0012
(440) 250-9117 fax
www.stampersanonymous.com

< ♘ > *Stamps used on pages 76, 79, 80*

❧☞ EYELETS, SOLID HEADS, BRADS, TYPEWRITER KEY RINGS, MICA TILES

Coffee Break Design
P.O. Box 34281
Indianapolis, IN 46234
(800) 229-1824 fax

❧☞ GOLDEN MEDIUMS, PAINTS, MOLDING PASTES, LIQUID ACRYLICS

Golden Artist Colors, Inc.
188 Bell Rd.
New Berlin, NY 13411
(607) 847-6154
www.goldenpaints.com

❧☞ DIAMOND GLAZE, STAMPS, LEAFING PENS *(gold, copper, silver)*

JudiKins
17803 South Harvard Blvd.
Gardena, CA 90248
(310) 515-1115
(310) 323-6619 fax
www.judikins.com

< ♘ > *Stamps used on pages 2, 6, 8, 14, 18, 38, 79, 96, 99, 100, 103, 104, 120, 121, 122, 123*

❧☞ OMNI GEL

Houston Arts, Inc.
10770 Moss Ridge Rd.
Houston, TX 77043
www.bearingbeads.com

❧☞ MICROGLAZE

Skycraft Designs, Inc.
26395 South Morgan Rd.
Estacada, OR 97023
(503) 630-7173 or (800) 578-5608
www.skycraft.com

❧☞ POLYMER CLAY, TISSUE BLADES, ACRYLIC ROLLING PINS

Polyform Products Co., Inc.
1901 Estes Ave.
Elk Grove, IL 60007
(847) 427-0020
www.sculpey.com

❧☞ BEESWAX, PIÑATA COLORS

Rupert, Gibbon & Spider, Inc.
P.O. Box 425
Healdsburg, CA 95448
(800) 442-0455
(707) 433-4906 fax
www.jacquardproducts.com

❧☞ PIÑATA COLORS, CLARO EXTENDER, MICA TILES, CHIPS AND GLITTER

USArtquest
7800 Ann Arbor Rd.
Grass Lake, MI 49240
(517) 522-6225
(517) 522-6228 fax
www.usartquest.com

❧☞ PAPER FOIL EPHEMERA

Amy's Magic Leaf
173 Main St.
West Leechburg, PA 15656
(724) 845-1748

❧☞ GAME PIECE EMBELLISHMENTS

Wonderland Emporium, Inc.
Boca Raton, FL 33432
(561) 395-6393
www.mystampstore.com

❧☞ VARIOUS STAMPS

Queen of Stamps
email: queenstamp@aol.com

< ♘ > *Stamps used on pages 34, 116, 119*

River City Rubber Works
5555 South Meridian
Wichita, KS 67217
(877) 735-2276
(316) 529-8940
www.rivercityrubberworks.com

< ♘ > *Stamp used on page 49*

Rubbermoon Stamp Company
P.O. Box 3258
Hayden Lake, ID 83835
(208) 772-9772
(208) 772-0701 fax
www.rubbermoon.com

< ♘ > *Stamps used on pages 88, 96, 99*

Stampington & Company
22992 Mill Creek, Ste. B
Laguna Hills, CA 92653
(877) STAMPER
www.stampington.com

< ♘ > *Stamp used on page 107*

Stampland
5033 N. Mozart Street
Chicago, IL 60625
(773) 293-0403

< ♘ > *Stamps used on pages 91, 119*

INDEX

GET CREATIVE WITH
NORTH LIGHT BOOKS!

THE ESSENTIAL GUIDE TO MAKING HANDMADE BOOKS

Gabrielle Fox teaches you how to create your own handmade books—one-of-a-kind art pieces—that go beyond the standard definition of what a "book" can be. You'll find 11 projects inside. Each one builds upon the next, just as your skills increase. This beginner-friendly progression ensures that you're well prepared to experiment, play and design your own unique, handmade books.

ISBN 1-58180-019-3, PAPERBACK, 128 PAGES, #31652-K

HOW TO BE CREATIVE IF YOU NEVER THOUGHT YOU COULD

Let Tera Leigh act as your personal craft guide and motivator. She'll help you discover just how creative you really are. You'll explore eight exciting crafts through 16 fun, fabulous projects, including rubber stamping, bookmaking, papermaking, collage, decorative painting and more. Tera prefaces each new activity with insightful essays and encouraging advice.

ISBN 1-58180-293-5, PAPERBACK, 128 PAGES, #32170-K

THE BIG BOOK OF GREETING CARDS

This book presents a variety of fun, festive and stylish ideas for making cards perfect for any occasion. Discover more than 40 step-by-step projects using a wide range of techniques including rubber stamping, stenciling, quilling and embroidery.

ISBN 1-58180-323-0, PAPERBACK, 144 PAGES, #32287-K

STENCILING & EMBOSSING GREETING CARDS

Judy Barker introduces you to the basics of stenciling and embossing attractive greeting cards. You'll also learn how to embellish them with foil, polymer clay, shrink plastic and more. It's everything you need to make one-of-a-kind cards for family and friends alike.

ISBN 0-89134-997-9, PAPERBACK, 128 PAGES, #31613-K

THESE AND OTHER FINE NORTH LIGHT TITLES ARE AVAILABLE FROM YOUR LOCAL ART & CRAFT RETAILER, BOOKSTORE, ONLINE SUPPLIER OR BY CALLING 1-800-448-0915.